12/7

D1716418

*To Lena*

GIANLUCA ZAGHI

# VINTAGE BICYCLES

## HOW TO FIND AND RESTORE OLD CYCLES

**MONDADORI**

# TABLE
# OF CONTENTS

# THE PRIDE OF PUTTING ITALY BACK AT THE CENTER OF THE WORLD

*Giancarlo Brocci*

—

Inventor and founder of the Eroica

My love of cycling dates back to the days of bottle caps and Vittorio Adorni. But it was first and foremost a passion as a *suiveur* and literary person, never as a cyclist, in my childhood: too many dangers for an only child suffering from poor health.

I soon began organizing cycling, but the Eroica was born when I still couldn't register with the platoon of enthusiasts. At the end of the past century, a torn cruciate ligament put an end to my last, modest soccer exploits, so I began pedaling. With no big ambitions, and the conviction of someone who knows that competing would be impossible, but soon realizes that the bicycle could give me so much unexpected gratification, starting from the boost to my self-esteem and manifest well-being. And then there's just one thing that can improve as a person ages: resilience, the endowment of long-standing cyclists.

All this to introduce an emblematic story, besides the true meaning behind this beautiful book. In 2003, three years after I had started taking up, slowly to be sure, many long-distance races, I decided to try out the adventure of the Paris-Brest-Paris, the Olympiad of bicycle touring, starting from its qualifying trials. Already on the road to Ville Lumière I met an engineer from Castelfiorentino who would end up accompanying me and my designated friend on the 1,225 km of the task. Along the way we talked about everything, and the first topic wasn't the bicycle, in the pure university spirit of nights spent following the rear lights of bicycles, red fireflies in the dark. But he already knew the Eroica and its inventor; it was still something small, today we would call it a "niche" phenomenon, and he suggested

going to see him. His mechanic had a warehouse full of old bicycles and he needed to empty it out because there was a good chance he could rent it. I think that no more than about ten days had gone by since we'd returned, after our titanic achievement of seventy-seven hours and seven minutes to make it back in triumph to Paris. I called him about paying him and his mechanic a visit. "You can see me whenever you want, but for the bicycles it's too late, he cut them all in half because he needed to make room." That was in 2003: it seems like a century has gone by since then. The Eroica was born just before, the idea and the culture that it spread, at first slowly, then with a powerful effect also thanks to the media boom, have allowed for the formidable recovery of a heritage. Others better than me will speak of what we were able to rediscover in these recent times and all around the world. The last one I cycled in was the Eroica Japan, where I was able to browse through the sacred texts concerning the history of gears, which will need to be translated since they're only available in Japanese, curated by the passion of local collectors. Naturally, the phenomenon has also been enriched by many online sales, auctions, and, why not, fakes; hard to establish how many bicycles belonging to Bartali and Coppi have seen the light, impossible to establish to what extent certain quotations are pertinent to the actual values of the items. For sure, what's considered heritage today is what the Eroica turned into value. The fact that it has put Italy, the history written by its champions, and its great craftsmanship, at the center of a world, fills us with pride.

INTRODUCTION

# WHEN MY LIFE HAS TAKEN A TURN
# THERE WAS A BICYCLE AT THE PIVOT POINT

*Mike Wolfe*
—

A collector of old bicycles, his show *American Pickers* has turned him into an international TV star

When Luca asked me to help introduce his book to American readers, my first thought was, no, because what could I possibly write that these beautiful photographs don't already say?

But bicycles have been a part of my life as long as I can remember. An old rusty carcass of a two-wheeler caught my eye when I was five years old... it turned out to be the first pick of a little boy who grew up to make a life and a world as a picker. And whether they took me to school in the mornings or on great adventures in the afternoons, bikes have been part of my life ever since. More than transportation, they've somehow been right there at many of my defining moments.

So my second thought was, yes, I can encourage readers to dive in. Not into my story, but into Luca's. I'm just here with this little welcome mat ...

For fourteen-year-old boys in Bettendorf, Iowa, in the late 1970s, life revolved around girls, football, bikes and stereos. I was 4'11" and 87 pounds, so football, and most girls, were off the table. But I had a passion for bikes, a succession of small part-time jobs and the unwavering single-mindedness of a true nerd. Every dime I earned and every spare minute I had in those days went toward finding and buying the parts to hand-build my real Italian bicycle.

With its authentic Campagnolo gruppo, it was sexy, exotic, high performance. On that bike, I was a racer, an athlete, the romantic lead. I could ride across Iowa on the RAGBRAI. I was the star of my own version of *Breaking Away*. My size was an advantage. I could fly.

Time after time in the years since, when my life has taken an unexpected turn there was a bicycle at the pivot point. And there are millions and millions of people who, when they stop to think, have stories like mine.

In this wonderful book, new admirers will see the amazing journey Luca has taken with these incomparable bicycles. And for seasoned aficionados, these images will bring back the glory of flying on these magical two-wheeled machines.

# HOW I GOT STARTED

Above and on the previous
page, Gianluca Zaghi in his
workshop.

There may be lots of different reasons why you're leafing through these pages. Maybe the fact that, in 2017, the bicycle celebrated its two hundredth anniversary encouraged you to buy this book. Or maybe you found an old bike in your cellar and you want to restore it. Maybe you cycle regularly, and have recently become interested in vintage bicycles. Or maybe you're just curious and have always loved beautiful things. More simply, maybe you just like photography, or you enjoy "getting your hands dirty."

Whatever your personal reason, you'll discover that the world you are about to approach is a truly special one.

For the past few years we have witnessed the revival of the bicycle, which is going through a new Golden Age. The change that's underway can clearly be felt in cities, in people's habits, in society. Traffic and pollution, the cost of fuel and the economic crisis, but also a policy that's focused on sustainable mobility have all determined a revolution aimed at a return to slowness. In the words of the French sociologist Marc Augé: "The bicycle is the magic potion that is now in the West's hands as it seeks to rediscover its urban happiness." This is a statement that I am happy to subscribe to.

In 2016, in some countries the number of new bicycles sold exceeded that of automobiles for the first time, a sign of profound social transformation where bicycles are playing an essential role. On TV, in print, at the movies… today the bicycle is everywhere. It's *fashionable*.

The bicycle has always played an important role in society, but I think that today it's even more significant, to the extent that it influences decisions made in the planning of urban infrastructures. Mobility inside and outside the city is enriched with cycle paths, and bikes feature prominently in the plans the most farsighted politicians and architects concoct to transform the way we move from A to B. Suffice to think of Norman Foster and his idea of a bicycle highway right in the city of London. This may still be a utopia today, but what about the future? "Bike-itecture," that is to say, the idea of bicycle-friendly building, is already a reality in many countries, and the trend is on the rise.

The bicycle is a simple means of transportation, within everyone's reach, but at the same time there's something magical about it, maybe because it was part of everyone's childhood. The joy that is felt when staying in balance on a two-wheeler, that feeling of freedom, independence, the wind blowing in your face: these emotions are inextricably linked to the first ride on this splendid object.

**Birth of a passion**   We live in a "liquid" world, where grasping something, tasting it, is becoming increasingly complicated. We are constantly on the go and it seems as though we never have enough time to stop. We have replaced working with our hands with working with a single finger, in the sense that life "scrolls" before us without our being able to appreciate each moment. Bombarded as we are by everything, we find it hard to grow fond of anything; we rarely show our emotions or reactions of wonder, everything leaves us indifferent.

There is an antidote to all this, and that antidote is passion. But passion requires love, devotion, constancy, and it has to be cultivated. It calls for participation, effort, commitment, and, above all, it calls for time. Besides, passion is good for you, even when it risks turning into an obsession.

I personally found this passion in bicycles; the fact that it later became an occupation is of secondary importance. For it is and always will be first and foremost a passion, because doing something passionately even makes hard work enjoyable.

My approach to the world of bicycle restoration came about by chance and, in a certain sense, by necessity. A few years ago, when I found myself out of work and with lots of time on my hands, I accepted a friend's invitation to go on some bike rides with him. At the time, I didn't have a bike, nor could I afford to buy a new one. It was my friend who suggested I search for a used one, and soon afterwards I bought a Moser road bike online at a bargain price. I was attracted more to the label than to the bike itself. As a child, Francesco Moser had been my idol, and my passion for cycling surfaced in the late 1970s, while watching him on TV as he won those three Paris-Roubaix races in a row.

When the bike finally arrived, I remember spending hours looking at it, full of admiration. I instantly realized that I could improve it with a few aesthetic tricks, and that was the spark that gave me the idea to devote my time to restoration. In the months that followed, I discovered a whole new world that up until then had been unknown to me, a world made up of remarkable people, endless anecdotes, dust-covered beauties.

A passion was born, and my hope is that you too will be infected by it.

# STORIES AND ASSESSMENTS

1

BiCi DA
TURISMO
O ciág!

BiCi DA CORSA

BiCi DA
CRONOMETRO

"M T B"
BiCi DA MONTAGNA

TYPES OF BICYCLES:

— TOURING BIKE
— ROAD BIKE
— TIME TRIAL BIKE
— MOUNTAIN BIKE

Previous page: Carlo Zanotta,
the heart and soul of CAT, an
amateur cycling group in Ticino,
wearing his Molteni jersey.

T here are many fascinating phases when restoring a bicycle. One of these is searching for a particular bicycle. This sort of "treasure hunt" is one of the things that intrigues me the most, it makes me feel like the Indiana Jones of two-wheelers. Because I'm curious, I've always enjoyed rummaging through the junk in the garage or in the attic to discover that hidden gem amid the dust and the rust, forgotten by all, but ready to be dug out, to be rescued. I must confess that all the different phases that went into my approach to certain bicycles were usually more interesting and more beautiful than the discovery itself.

**Stories, discoveries, and research** Another moment I love is the one that's linked to the stories, to the events that hide behind each bicycle. Doing this kind of work you have the good fortune of meeting a lot of interesting, special people who are in love with two-wheelers. Many of them are a precious source of information that's hard to find elsewhere, a historic memory to be safeguarded just like the bicycles themselves.

Sometimes it takes very little to create a story. For example, even a T-shirt might do the trick. That's what happened when I found one inscribed with words in my local Canton Ticino dialect: "I girin da la dumeniga" (short Sunday rides). It was obviously the name of an amateur cycling group. My interest was piqued to the point that I started doing research into the various local cycling clubs, and after a few months this led me to the discovery of CAT – Ciclismo Amatoriale Ticinese (Ticino Amateur Bicycle Club). What put me on their trail was a woollen shirt that I often saw hanging in the various repair shops and bicycle stores where I hang out because of my work. My interest to learn more about it and my perseverance led me to another fascinating discovery. While talking to me about this particular club, former racers or mechanics often mentioned a certain Mr. Zanotta, who was apparently its heart and soul (they say he used to go to bed wearing his woollen shirt and cycling cap!). I discovered that he had collected quite a number of bicycles, all of which rather unique,

and with the information at my disposal, as well as a pinch of luck, I managed to dig up about a dozen of the masterpieces that had belonged to his fantastic collection. They were all quality bicycles, emblematic of the excellence of Italian production in the 1970s and 1980s, with names like Colnago, De Rosa, Magni, Moser, Motta, Benotto, Freschi... It was an honor for me to rediscover them and submit them to conservative restoration. Putting my hands on those masterpieces was a lesson in the design and history of some of the greatest Italian bicycle makers of that day and age.

Curiosity and a thirst for information are indispensable ingredients for this type of discovery.

Another unique and eccentric character who I am glad to remember was Mr. Vassalli, a little old man who was a genius and had a passion for bikes. A cyclist friend introduced us, and when I went to visit him at his home I soon realized that I was in some sort of museum: bicycles, motorcycles, motorbikes, and tricycles heaped up in every corner. He kindly offered me a cup of coffee and before actually showing me his masterpieces, he let me look at a few pictures of them that he had carefully put together in small photo albums. I was astonished at the passion in his voice as he described his bikes even before showing them to me. Although he was over seventy, as he told me about his hobby his eyes were those of a happy child. He was very jealous of everything he'd managed to collect, and he was thinking of starting a museum. He took me to see his whole house, showing me everything he'd succeeded in collecting over the years: there were rooms and a garage filled with bicycles, apparently piled together haphazardly, with no rhyme or reason, but actually stowed away lovingly and often protected by big blankets or dust sheets. Each time he lifted one of those drapes a whole world opened up before me. Hidden beneath the dust, I noticed a saddle with the name of my city on it. I asked him if I might have it. When our meeting ended, to my amazement, I found he had put it inside my car.

A decal is instead the common thread in this other curious anecdote. I had run into a frame with an adhesive label that read "tarantella." At

Above: Original cycling jersey
for the amateur group "I girin
da la dumeniga"; notice the
picture of Bartali wearing the
same jersey.

Right: The interior of the
author's workshop.

the time I didn't pay much attention to it, but that name kept going around in my head. I started asking my friends and former cyclists about it, until one of them, a former semi-professional, told me this story, which was later confirmed by others. "Tarantella" was the name of a Ticino night club that was the haunt of racers and cyclists; the owner had even decided to sponsor a semi-professional team.

If at times a mere label can hide a piece of history, at other times a normal conversation can bring out a masterpiece. That was the case for a 1976 orange Colnago that I found after talking to a friend about the things I loved the most. Her father kept this gem in the basement and he even still had the original invoice, something that's extemely rare!

One day the owner of one of the bicycle repair and sales stores that I work with asked me if I wanted to buy an old light green Priori. The bicycle was in satisfactory condition and as soon as I got home I started fixing it. The following morning when I went out to buy the material I needed to do so, while I was waiting at the traffic light, I noticed a pickup truck with a bicycle sticking out of the rear loading area along with some other things that looked like they were part of a move. At the next traffic light I pulled up alongside it and asked the driver if the bicycle was by any chance for sale. All I could see was a part of the handlebar, enough to tell me that it was a quality item. The handlebar cover was made of leather, typical of top-of-the-line bicycle parts. We pulled over into a parking lot and agreed on the price,

Below: Florio Cappelletti,
the owner, in the 1930s,
of a famous bicycle store
in Mendrisio (Switzerland).

Right: Team sponsored by
Florio (standing in the middle).

1936. Gruppo Florio Mendrisio.

then I put the bicycle into my car. This was also a Priori, a baby blue one, and I thought what a strange coincidence it was to find two such bikes in just two days. I was even more amazed when, as I was telling my best friend about my discovery, it came out that the baby blue one was most likely his father's bike, which his mother had thrown out not too long ago at the waste depot.

For the first time ever, it dawned on me that whenever I go out looking for bicycles I'm surrounded by a special energy… I got proof of this that very evening. While I was having dinner in the usual neighborhood family-run restaurant, I told the owner, who I was having a chat with, the story about the Priori. His sister, who was sitting close to our table, was listening in on our conversation, and when we had finished talking she told me that her father had one in the cellar. For a second there I thought she was pulling my leg, but then I realized she was dead serious. So a few days later I went to pick up my third Priori, this one yellow, and of the three unquestionably the best-looking.

A dear friend named Walter, a super-enthusiast when it comes to vintage bicycles, came to see me one morning with a 1960s Cinelli that he had just found near my house. I was taken aback, especially because in the four years I had spent looking I hadn't managed to find one with that trademark. I was enthralled by the beauty of the bicycle, and at the same time envious and sort of angry with myself for not having been the one to track it down.

It was a stupid attitude, I have to admit, but it was probably what led to the discovery I was to make soon afterwards. I immediately started phoning all the former racers whose numbers I had in my phone book to find out if anyone had a forgotten Cinelli somewhere in the cellar, and one of them said he did. It was in his garage and had been gathering dust for some time. That same day I went to see him and was blown away when in his garage, in the midst of about a dozen bicycles hanging vertically and sort of pushed together to make room for a couple of cars, I glimpsed a Cinelli Laser Strad practically in mint condition. I remember asking him in a whisper whether it was for sale. He replied that he had to ask his son, and I thought to myself, "goodbye Cinelli," a dream gone up in smoke. But instead, to my amazement, his son agreed to the sale. On my way back home with the bicycle in my car I thought about how full of surprises life can be.

We live in a hyperconnected world, constantly bombarded by images and experiences of all sorts that the social networks reflect and disseminate in real time. It is undeniable that all these bits and pieces of information contribute to expanding what we know and, especially when our passions are at stake, all you need is a simple photograph to uncork endless discussions, exchanges of opinions, comments. Not too long ago on a social network I ran into a picture posted by a Californian representing a cycling team from the 1930s called Ciclo Florio. I recognized

A 1983 Cinelli Laser Strada.

Above: Badges and transfer decals
for the Ciclo Florio sent to me
by Judd, Florio's grandson, now
living in California.

On pp. 28-31: A 1930s
Brunotto, an example
of conservative restoration.

the picture right away, seeing that I had classified it as one of the most beautiful images of vintage cycling in my region. Ciclo Florio was a shop in Mendrisio, not too far from where I live, that sold bicycles and velocipedes in the 1930s. Curious about how a Californian could have ended up with such a picture, I checked his profile and discovered that his name was Judd Cappelletti, grandson of Florio Cappelletti, who was the owner of the shop back then. Surprised by the coincidence, I got in touch with Judd and we had a long talk about his grandfather and cycling in general. What he told me was amazing: his grandfather had left him a trunk filled with history, memories, beauty; the recollections of a life entirely devoted to making bicycles and cycling.

Photos, patents, receipts... and metal badges, decals, paint tests, all 1930s and 1940s originals, and Judd had lovingly preserved it and generously decided to share it with the world through the internet by opening a dedicated website (www.cicloflorio.com). In Mendrisio there's nothing left of that small shop today, and what Judd preserves in his trunk in California is a unique and precious witness to a piece of the heroic cycling of the past. Incidentally, Judd kindly sent me three original metal badges and several reproductions of old decals.

Although this is just a small example, it is useful to help us understand how the Internet can also act as a crucial tool to retrieve information that can help with the restoration of vintage bicycles.

Above: A Masi Ferretti Team
photographed when it was first found.

Right: An example of the initial
conditions of a front wheel.

**Evaluation of the original conditions** Though often underestimated or even overlooked, one of the most important things that has to be done when you begin working to restore a bike is to carefully evaluate its initial conditions. An in-depth examination of its state of conservation is essential to determine what you can expect in terms of work, time, and cost, and it will help avoid unforeseen complications along the way that could force you to leave the work unfinished. And since old bicycles are usually found in cramped, poorly-lit places it's best to know what you're looking for, and where to look.

First of all, you need to identify the year of production. The evaluation criteria will in fact differ if you're dealing with a bicycle from the 1930s or one from the 1980s. Faced with a very old bike you can expect the frame to be only just acceptable, especially as concerns the paint, while in the case of a newer bike you can expect its conditions to be better overall. After having established the period of manufacture as accurately as possible, divide the bike into two large sec-

tions, the frame and the components, and pro-ceed to examine both of them methodically and meticulously.

**The frame** The first thing you need to do is check to see if there is any unsightly damage to the frame, for example, dents or cracks visible to the naked eye. You then proceed to check the geometries (a vise does the job best). You try to understand if the bicycle has been involved in an accident, especially the front. It doesn't take much to see whether the fork has been damaged. The best way to do that is to turn the handlebar and spin the front wheel.

Then you move on to check some sensitive parts, such as the the brazed parts, if present, both those for the cable housings and those for the de-railleurs, the bottom bracket shell, the rear drop-out and the seat binder, where you'll see wheth-er there is any damage to the seatpost or to the bridge for the closing binder bolt.

Once the structural test is complete, you can move on to the aesthetic check-up, evaluating the

condition of the paint. Establishing whether a frame needs to be repainted is important with a view to calculating the costs. You generally consider the presence of scratches, rust, peeling, or blisters, taking care to examine the bicycle both from above and below. In the case of delicate paint jobs like *cromovelato* and nickel-plating, check to see if there are any typical discolorations and tarnishing. The same goes for the single chrome parts, where you often come across the greatest concentration of rust: it can be on the surface, or else it may have badly corroded the metal.

Once the paint has been checked, focus on the decals. They generally have a significant aesthetic impact and their condition greatly influences the final evaluation. Make sure there are no detachments or abrasions due to heat or humidity, and check to see whether they match the model and the brand of the bicycle, because it is rather common to come across inconsistencies due to prior replacements.

In general, the presence of scratches due to normal wear and tear and a certain patina on the paint are to be deemed acceptable and actually contribute to creating that "lived-in" effect that I rather like myself. If you have any doubts, you mustn't be too hasty in deciding to repaint a frame, but should take your time before making a final decision once you've dismantled and looked at the single parts of the bicycle and above all after you've cleaned it carefully. More than once I changed my mind right after cleaning, which can work miracles at times.

Besides the frame it's very important to analyze the wheels, which have a considerable aesthetic impact. Check the match between the front and rear wheels and the state of the different component parts: rims, spokes, hubs, skewers, and tires. Bear in mind that if you need to replace any of these it's not always so easy to find the right parts. Check the spokes in particular, to see whether any are missing and the state of those that still exist. If they're rusty they'll look bad, and will definitely have to be replaced. To judge the good working of the wheels, let them spin, possibly after removing them from the frame, to see whether they have been damaged or need tuning.

Once the examination of the frame and the wheels has been completed, we already have some idea of the bicycle's general conditions. What we have to do now is examine the components, the so-called "white parts."

**The components** Before checking the aesthetic and functional conditions of a bicycle's components, it's a good idea to go ahead with an analysis of their historical compliance, establishing whether each piece is original, that is, if it dates back to the same period of the bicycle's production or whether it was replaced. This procedure presupposes a knowledge of the leading brands at least in general terms, and the types of groups marketed in the various eras, a skill that is acquired with time and experience. That historical evaluation is of essential importance if you want to go ahead with a conservative restoration, while it instead becomes a secondary factor if you want to carry out a "creative" restoration.

The examination of the components can be subdivided into two phases. The first one focuses on the pieces made from perishable materials, like rubber, cloth, leather, and even wood. Then you check on the state of the wear and tear of the cable gear set, the saddle, the handlebar tape, the brake pads, the laces of the toe-clips straps, and any bags or wooden rims. In the second one the focus is on the state of the iron and steel or aluminum parts, paying attention in the first case to the rust and the chrome plating, and in the second to the level of oxidation, the state of anodization, and the presence of any cracks.

An aesthetic evaluation is simple enough for anyone, while the functional evaluation can be slightly more difficult.

A delicate component is the seatpost. If there's rust or oxidation, or if it hasn't been greased regularly in the course of time, it may turn out to be difficult to remove.

To test the working of the steering unit, as it will be rather hard to dismantle it during the preliminary examination to carefully look at the state of the ball bearings, it may be useful, after having removed the front wheel, to turn the fork to the right and to the left to feel whether it moves smoothly or whether there are any jams. The same applies to the bottom bracket, for which you can simply turn the crank arm, after having momentarily removed the chain, and the pedals, paying attention to any jams or jerks of the ball bearings. As for the pedals you also need to make sure that they have their dust caps, which are not easy to replace if they're missing. Let's take a quick look at the chain as well, considering the fact that it's normal to replace it when it's worn or rusty.

Another important component that needs to be tested is the freewheel: to evaluate whether it flows properly producing its characteristic (and

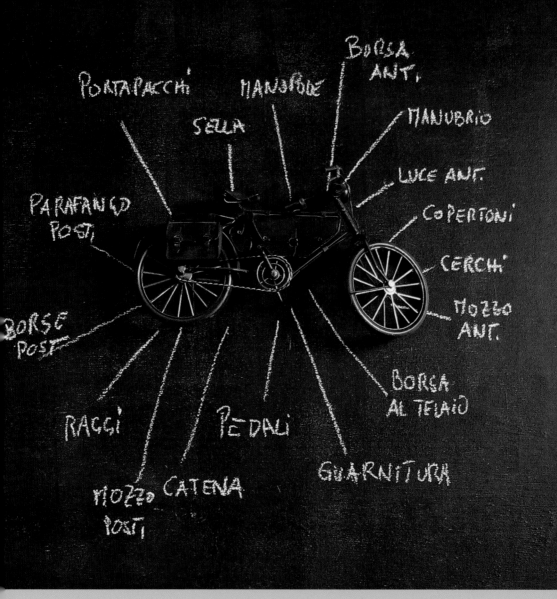

PORTAPACCHI

BORSA ANT.

MANOPOLE

SELLA

MANUBRIO

LUCE ANT.

PARAFANGO POST

COPERTONI

CERCHI

MOZZO ANT.

BORSE POST

BORSA AL TELAIO

RAGGI

PEDALI

GUARNITURA

MOZZO POST

CATENA

## THE BASIC BICYCLE COMPONENTS
(Clockwise from the top)

- BREAK LEVERS
- HANDLEBAR GRIPS
- HANDLEBAR BAG
- FRONT LIGHT
- FRONT BRAKE
- TIRES
- FRONT HUB

- FRONT FENDER
- FRAME
- RIGHT CRANK ARM
  AND CHAINRINGS
- PEDALS
- CHAIN
- REAR HUB

- SPOKES
- RIMS
- REAR FENDER
- REAR DOUBLE
  PANNIER BAGS
- REAR CARRIER
- SADDLE

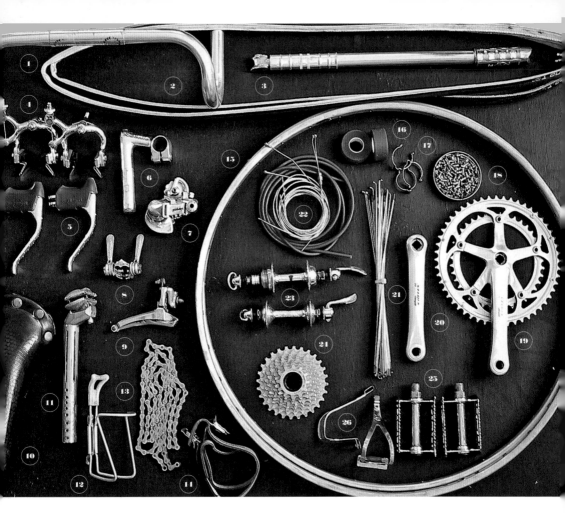

# THE COMPONENTS OF A RACING BICYCLE

1 . HANDLEBAR

2 . TUBULARS

3 . PUMP

4 . BRAKE CALIPERS

5 . BRAKE LEVERS

6 . STEM

7 . REAR DERAILLEUR

8 . DOWNTUBE SHIFTERS LEVERS

9 . FRONT DERAILLEUR

10 . SADDLE

11 . SEATPOST

12 . WATER BOTTLE HOLDER

13 . CHAIN

14 . TOE-CLIPS STRAPS

15 . RIMS

16 . HANDLEBAR TAPE

17 . CABLE GEAR CLIPS

18 . SPOKE NIPPLES

19 . RIGHT SIDE CRANK ARM WITH CHAINRINGS

20 . LEFT SIDE CRANK ARM

21 . SPOKES

22 . CABLE GEAR SET

23 . HUBS

24 . FREEWHEEL

25 . PEDALS

26 . TOE-CLIPS

# TOURING BICYCLE ACCESSORIES

1 . CYCLOTOURIST
    HANDLEBAR BAG

2 . REAR ALUMINUM
    TOOL BAGS

3 . BELL

4 . TIRE TUBE CAGE

5 . SEATPOST SADDLE CLAMP

6 . SEATPOST

7 . PUMP AND PUMP CLIP

8 . CHAINGUARD

9 . TOURIST HANDLEBAR

10 . DURALUMINUM FENDERS

11 . TOURIST SADDLE

12 . OLD HEROIC TOURIST
     SUNGLASSES

13 . TOURIST WATER BOTTLE
     (750 CL)

14 . REVERSE BRAKE LEVERS

15 . FRONT LIGHT

16 . SMALL REAR LIGHT

17 . REAR LIGHT AND REFLECTOR

18 . REAR REFLECTOR

19 . DYNAMO

20 . DYNAMO CABLE

Magni Ferrari ICS with ICS Zurigo group, which
transformed the components of the Campagnolo
into a luxury version, visible in the detail of the gear
levers on the opposite page.

pleasing) buzz, suffice to hold it blocked with one
hand while you spin the wheel.

As regards the brakes, check the calipers (including the presence of the brake adjuster) and
the levers (by pulling them you can see whether
the springs are working properly), and then the
state of the pads and the rubber lever hoods. These
parts are highly subject to wear and very likely
need replacing.

If the bike has gears, we should also consider
the conditions of the front and the rear derailleurs,
as well as the shifting levers. Their congruence is
of essential importance, i.e. they must belong to
the same set; quite often you come across mixed
up situations, as a result of successive and partial
replacements.

Moving on to the handlebar and the stem, you
need to check their integrity, the state of the rust
and, in the case of the stem, the fact that there
are no cracks in the most delicate parts where the
handlebar is attached.

The grips will probably be worn as well,
whether they're made of plastic, bone, bakelite, or
any other material. Let's check to see if they can
be restored; if not, with a bit of luck we might
find some replacements in the flea markets or
on the Internet. For the tape, on the other hand,
if it needs replacing, bear in mind that today it
can generally be found easily in different colors
and types; even the handlebar covers made from
hand-stitched leather can easily be remade in that,
seeing the boom in the demand for vintage bikes,
some specialized companies have started manufacturing them again.

Lastly, when you're dealing with a bike with
accessories, pay special attention to the condition
of the fenders and chainguard, both of which are
very delicate and often damaged. Similarly, painting, chrome plating, and any decals are also likely
to be in poor condition. The latter should be evaluated carefully as a new paint job will affect the
overall budget.

# ARTISANAL SKILLS AND DESIGN
# DEDICATED TO THE BICYCLE

*Helio Ascari*

—

Designer and maker of Ascari Bicycles in Brooklyn, New York

I never went to school to study design or anything. I was 11 years old when I started working in steel and wood factories, and the fact that I was surrounded by people with such amazing knowledge and skills helped me understand design and fabrication. Later, after 13 years working in the fashion industry, I decided to work with my very first passion: bicycles. I love to build something from scratch and combine the timeless sense of beauty with sophisticated design.

When I started developing Ascari Bicycles, I was bringing everything from my past, and my Italian heritage. The name Ascari always pulsed inside of me, and gave me determination and courage to write my own story. I grew up in an Italian village in the south of Brazil, and everything I had surrounding me was old objects that the immigrants brought from Italy. I was always fascinated by the durability of those pieces, the time it takes to make them, the passion in the beautiful details, and the quality of

the materials. There was a substantial soul attached to them. This is exactly what I like to bring to my bicycles. I am attached to the beauty, the passion and the craft that existed in the old days.

In the beginning I wasn't planning on developing something that intricate, I was honestly putting out a strong desire to build something unique, and that desire was a pure manifestation of my heart. On the other hand, my mind always believed that the mastery of a craft is demonstrated by outstanding precision, attention to detail and remarkable finishes, and that was what I wanted to translate into my creations.

I believe that the challenge of design is to create a bicycle that can be part of your living room yet also be a tool for a more sustainable planet. I have a fascination with such a simple machine that helps us to move forward using only our energy. This machine is a testament to both my company's design philosophies and, quite simply, elevates bicycle construction to an art form. I like to think that a bicycle is a design object I build with the precision of a goldsmith that will be transmitted from generation to generation.

I build my frames utilizing lugs and fillet brazing, producing a frame with an ageless style, I am dedicated to providing the best quality bicycle. I opt for a 1930s geometry for the King series, with a 68-degree head tube and seat tube, and long chain stays. I like to use classic Italian wooden rims 700c and I incorporate jewelry details in the building process. In addition to the bicycle frame, fork and stem I also hand-build some parts like brake levers from a combination of materials such as brass, bronze or aluminum depending on the project, exotic wood, leather, gold and precious gems.

Someone once wrote that the "King is to bicycles what the Bugatti Type 57SC Atlantic is to automobiles. Pure exorbitant rolling speed, built with only the rider in mind." I couldn't help but smile with an uppermost satisfaction and a realization that I was indeed able to use my passion and perseverance to express my vision symbolized by a bicycle.

# AIM AND
# CHOICE OF
# RESTORATION

A Colnago Super restored
according to the client's specific
requests.

**T**he bicycle is an aesthetically beautiful object; for many it's a work of art, even when it's covered in dust or rust. Restoring a bicycle is basically a process aimed at bringing its beauty out once again, returning the bicycle to its ancient splendor. But that's not all: getting one's hands dirty to restore a relic from the past can have a therapeutic effect as well. This is true of any type of manual labor, today more than ever, but it's particularly true for an activity like restoration. Seeing the immediate, concrete results of our efforts is rewarding and fills us with pride. Over the years, I have restored hundreds of bicycles to their ancient splendor, but above all I have given myself a new life. A life of satisfaction, special encounters, and fascinating discoveries.

The bicycle has recently celebrated its two hundredth anniversary and every single one that we bring back to life hides lots of small anecdotes worth telling. The two-wheeler holds within itself an entire world, a philosophy of life, a way of being. It is an object rich in design and innovation, but above all one that brims with history.

**Creative restoration** One of the first reasons that encourages many people to devote themselves to restoration work is the sheer pleasure they experience when they breathe new life into a long-forgotten object. This is what happens in what we might refer to as "creative restoration": making an old bicycle work again by being able to freely choose everything that can make it more beautiful so that we feel it's completely *ours*.

I've completed lots of restorations for friends and clients without following any historical reference, but with the sole aim of fulfilling their requests and desires.

As it has no particular restrictions, creative restoration can get under way from the frame alone, simply a skeleton on which to unleash your imagination and give free rein to your creativity. This type of restoration is useful as a sort of apprenticeship, it prepares you for more demanding experiences, like trying your hand at "historical" restoration aimed at preserving the original features of the bicycle and its value. This type of restoration calls for a completely different approach.

**History and collecting** Historical restoration, that is to say, the type of restoration that's done while keeping in mind the history of the bicycle that's being worked on, is unquestionably more complicated, and it also requires more time with respect to restoration that's carried out for pleasure. To do a job correctly it will first of all be necessary to research the original features of the brand and the model. Until little over a decade ago, this procedure might have been rather time-consuming. But today, thanks to the Internet and to the burgeoning of events devoted to vintage bicycles, it's a lot simpler. Trading exhibitions, garage and yard sales, and races along heroic routes are held on all five continents. This ferment has contributed to disseminating a passion for vintage, consequently making it easier for people to retrieve historical data. When I first started restoring bicycles I would never have imagined I would find myself faced with such a wealth of information. The more you get into it, the likelier it is you're going to want to read, discover facts, visit exhibitions and museums about bicycles so that you can compare your own work with and observe that of others.

It helps you to have a starting point, a reference and, why not, to improve yourself.

While it's true that we're living in a globalized world, we mustn't overlook the fact that a good place to start to gather information is the place we live in. Wherever you live, former cyclists, bike builders, and bike sellers are often the guardians of a rich and deeply rooted tradition. Talking to them is an absorbing experience and a must when you're doing restoration work. Knowledge that has been accumulated over the years is essential in this type of work, and the more we compare our own work with that of others, the better the final results are going to be. It's a non-stop learning process, and the pleasure and satisfaction that comes with actually doing the restoration work is an important part of it.

**Conservative or total?** When you restore a bicycle for the purpose of preserving its historic value, you need to choose between doing a conservative job and no more than that, or totally revamping the bicycle, including repainting the

Left: Example of creative restoration: I restored
this Ganna according to my personal taste,
modifying the original color and components.

Above: Example of the conservative restoration
of a De Rosa 30° Anniversario.

On pp. 50-53: A stunning example of an early 1970s
De Rosa. Note the leather saddle and tubular holder,
and the elegant handlebar cover, patented by Almarc
Lissone (MI).

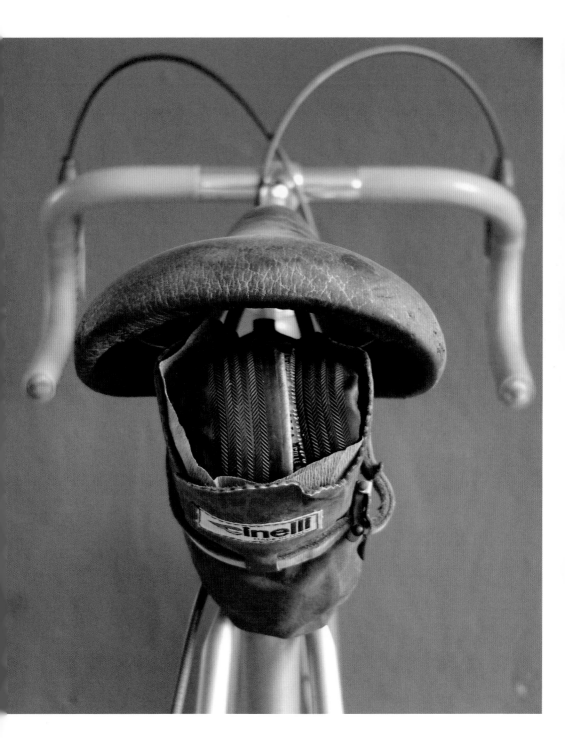

Bianchi frame that underwent total restoration. It had been poorly painted with bright orange spray paint that didn't correspond to the original Bianchi color.

Opposite: Example of conservative restoration of a Masi Ferretti Team. When I first found the bike, the wheels weren't from the period it was manufactured, but more recent. Luckily, the former owner had carefully preserved the original wheels with wooden rims, so the bicycle could be restored to its original condition.

frame. The decision is obviously a subjective one, but generally speaking, the conditions of the bicycle will help you decide. Repainting the frame means eliminating the lived-in charm that lingers in an antique object; somehow it devalues the bicycle.

If the person is a collector who also wants to preserve the economic value of the object, then conservative restoration should always be preferred over total conservation. If economic value isn't an issue, then the choice between conservative and total will be harder to make. As a rule of thumb, I suggest postponing the decision to after the frame has been thoroughly cleaned. Often, a good cleaning is sufficient to aesthetically revive the beauty of the paint.

If the choice is to repaint the bicycle, then you have to be sure you'll be able to locate the right decals for the brand and the model. Repainting a frame to then leave it anonymous doesn't make much sense. You should keep in mind that when certain decals are no longer available on the market, they can be reproduced by a graphic artist, although this will cost much more than a set that already exists. And don't forget: when buying decals, better to spend more and avoid problems later.

*Conservative restoration* is no doubt the most economical and the simplest to execute. By and large, it's also the type of restoration that doesn't require hiring outside professionals. With a bit of experience and enough time, this type of restoration is within everyone's reach.

However, although it's relatively simple, it's also the type of restoration that's the most prone to error, usually due to a lack of experience. Problems often arise during the cleaning phase, when over-abrasive detergents are chosen. At other times, it concerns the choice of components—cable gear sets, handlebar tape, and tires—whose importance is often mistakenly underestimated; such components may need to be replaced because they're worn or not from the same period. The rigorous collector will know how to replace such parts artfully. What's important is to not set limits when it comes to the research, which needs to be done before getting started. The more information you have about what the bicycle originally looked like, the fewer the errors and inconsistencies.

At times, you end up in a stalemate situation owing to the difficulties in retrieving the right component. This is especially the case with old bicycles from the 1920s or 1930s. The problem can be solved by looking for a replacement part that dates to the same period as the one that needs to be replaced. This is a compromise that can be resorted to when the work that's done is conservative.

Patience is of the essence in this type of restoration. Personally, I find that hunting for a particular piece is the beauty of this job. Research arouses never-ending discussions with friends and colleagues and takes you to visit exhibitions and sift through markets. You need lots of perseverance. And a pinch of luck.

And once you've achieved your goal, the satisfaction that fills the heart and the soul make up for all the effort you've put into the task. Not only are you breathing new life into a neglected object, but you're leaving the physical proof of its historical value for future generations.

*Total restoration*, unlike conservative restoration, is more complicated and more expensive.

It can also involve having to hire outside professionals, for instance, to repaint the frame, or to chrome some of the pieces. Before getting started it may be worthwhile finding out whether there are any painters or companies specialized in galvanic processes in the area where you live. Allow me to say that it's not easy to find someone who's good at painting bicycle frames. Resorting to a body shop for cars may be an affordable choice, but you need to take into account the fact that a person working in a body shop hardly ever has the right experience to paint a bicycle. On the other hand, a professional who routinely paints frames will probably be more expensive, but will do a perfect job.

In addition to the problem of the decals, which was discussed previously, when restoration is total the choice of color is of essential importance. The traces of the original paint that are still visible on the frame serve as an important reference. I suggest taking some small samples with you when you're ready to choose the color.

If a concrete reference is lacking, you'll find all the information you need online by googling the brand and the model. Many catalogues can be consulted electronically, and there are numerous forums and websites for enthusiasts that can help retrieve such data. As a rule, for the bicycles that are collected and restored the most, finding the exact color code even for periods in the past is not uncommon. If, instead, no information about color can be found, then as a basic reference you can exploit the range of colors used for car manufacturing.

Bicycles manufactured before the 1940s rarely feature metallic colors; during that period the range of colors was limited and dull. It was only in the decades that followed, especially in the 1970s and 1980s, that an almost endless range of colors became available. And you also need to remember that some of the painting processes of the past are hard to reproduce today; this should be kept in mind to avoid being disappointed. Lastly, when you're not sure what to do, it might be worthwhile asking the painter for advice.

**Costs** Once a certain type of restoration has been chosen, whether it be conservative or total, it is of key importance to get an idea of the overall cost in order to avoid unpleasant surprises. In most cases, conservative restoration is costly for the restorer in terms of the time and devotion that are required, while the products used for cleaning and the replacement parts won't be particularly expensive. Total restoration, on the other hand, can be costly, especially if some of the tasks need to be handed over to outside professionals, who should always be asked for estimates. That way you won't end up spending more

than the intrinsic value of the bike itself by the time the job is finished.

Here's another piece of advice: try to use artisans or professionals who work locally. If further finishings are required, or if you're unhappy with some part of the bicycle, you'll be close to where the work was done and will be able to handle the situation more easily.

You should also make a complete list of the component parts that you want or have to replace so that you can factor them into the overall estimate of the cost for the work at hand.

**Timing and planning** Once you've chosen the type of restoration and worked out the overall costs, it's a good idea to carefully plan all the phases that will lead to completion of the work and figure out exactly how long each of them will take. This will mean doing things in an orderly fashion and maximizing the timing. We often get carried away by our eagerness to do something, by the eagerness to see results instantly. But this way

of working can cause confusion and the target can move even farther out of reach. On the contrary, being well organized will help to make the various phases successful, especially if you're going to need outside help to get some of them done.

With time and experience, everyone will find their own personal methodology, and get used to making a plan depending on their needs. Organization, order, and planning are indispensable ingredients for getting good results, but, if the aim is the same for everyone, then it's right for everyone to evaluate what pattern suits him or her best. Part of what's exciting about restoring a bicycle is feeling that it's your very own project, and this can be accomplished if you adopt a personal method with your own techniques and solutions.

Later, as we talk more in-depth about the two types of restoration, conservative and total, I'll tell you about *my* working methods. These won't necessarily overlap with yours, but they may be useful as guidelines or as a benchmark to allow you to improve, if possible, your own way of working.

# THE CICLI FRATELLI ROSSI
# WORSKHOP AND MUSEUM

*Stelio Rossi*

—

Stelio Rossi, Ranieri Rossi's son, is currently in charge
of the Register of Heroic Bicycles.

In the heart of Siena, a stone's throw away from Piazza del Campo, is a piece of the history of heroic cycling that's a must-see for anyone who loves vintage bicycles. I'm referring to the Ranieri Rossi workshop and museum that has been installed on the corner of Via dell'Oliviera and Via Roma by Stelio Rossi, the last descendent of a glorious Sienese family of "bicycle-makers."

It was around the mid-1930s when the three brothers, Eugenio, Martino, and Ranieri Rossi, who already ran a bicycle repair and sales shop in Siena, decided to buy the Daveri bicycle repair shop located in the hamlet of Maddalena, which would especially benefit from Ranieri's workmanship. For four whole decades, the shop was a point of reference for Sienese and Tuscan cycling—from 1946 to 1953 the three brothers sponsored the Coppa F.lli Rossi (Rossi Brothers Cup), part of the Campionato Toscano Dilettanti (Tuscan Amateur Championship)— until the mid-1970s, when Ranieri decided to close the business and retire to the Sienese countryside.

After a few decades of oblivion, the shop was given a new life thanks to Stelio, who, inspired by his own love of cycling from the past, decided to share with heroic cycling enthusiasts the memory of a business that his father and uncles had devoted their entire lives to, and a means of transportation that had characterized Italy in the past century.

What's special about this store-museum is that the original interior has remained intact. The workbench, the tools, the equipment, the desk for the administrative work complete with ink blotter, stamps, telephone, and binders filled with orders and invoices are in the exact same place they used to be.

Enthusiasts and curiosity-seekers will appreciate the historic heritage within. The lavish original collection, later joined by important acquisitions and donations, includes a large number of bicycles that have been preserved or restored, advertising posters for the various brands from the past, cyclist's shirts and caps, saddles, bags, handlebar, pumps, gears, crank arms, freewheels, rims, hubs, spokes, bells, pedals, lights (candles, oil, acetylene, and dynamos), metal tags for a whole variety of brands, and other objects dating back to when the store was operating.

The knowledgable eye will especially be drawn to the racing gear, among which the following stand out: the Wolsit that the Milanese Enrico Sala rode in the 1909 Giro d'Italia, two Dei (1927 Milan-Sanremo and 1938 Marca Oro Corsa), five Bianchis (1938 Saetta, 1940 Folgore, 1950 Folgorissima, 1951 Paris-Roubaix, 1953 Tour de France), two Legnanos (1938 Corsa and 1960 Gran Premio), and a 1949 Arbos that belonged to the racing cyclist Primo Volpi.

Among the non-road bicycles, especially noteworthy are three pieces that came straight from the hands of the Rossi brothers: a 1946 tandem, a 1947 transport bike, and a transformable men's/women's bicycle produced that same year. Also worthy of mention are a late-nineteenth-century French bicycle, a 1923 Tuscan model, a 1923 Dei, a 1933 Bianchi, a 1933 Atala, a 1935 Dei (the first of its kind sold in the shop), an Airolg, a sub-brand of the 1936 Gloria (knife-grinder's bicycle), a 1938 Taurus, and a 1943 Maino Aerodyne.

A portrait of Fausto Coppi and Gino Bartali wrapped in the flags of the Sienese contrada (district) of Valdimontone as they get ready to head out for the fourth stage of the 1952 Giro d'Italia is perhaps the most appealing of the many period photographs adorning the walls.

A new gem has recently been added to this precious collection: an 1867 Michaux velocipede.

# THE WORKSHOP: PRODUCTS AND TOOLS

3

BREV. CAMPAG

BREV. INTER. CAMP

CAMPAGNOL

CAMPAGNOLO

BREV. INTER. CAMPAGNOLO

BREV. CAMPAGNOLO

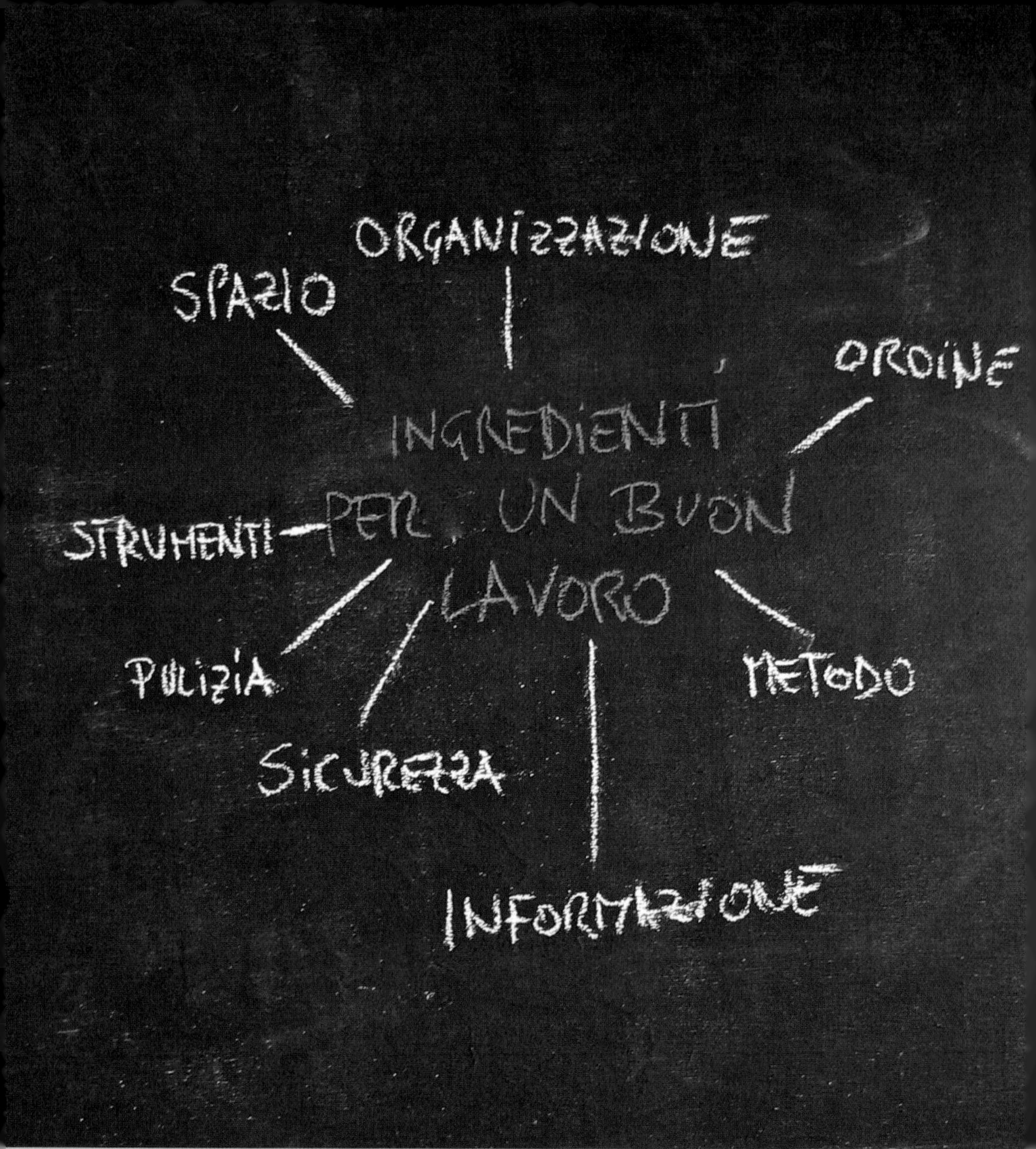

ORGANIZZAZIONE

SPAZIO

ORDINE

INGREDIENTI
PER UN BUON
LAVORO

STRUMENTI

PULIZIA

SICUREZZA

METODO

INFORMAZIONE

WHAT YOU WILL NEED IN THE WORKSHOP

THE INGREDIENTS FOR A GOOD JOB

– ORGANIZATION
– ORDER
– METHOD
– INFORMATION
– SAFETY
– CLEANLINESS
– TOOLS
– SPACE

reparing and setting out a space where you can cultivate your passion is one of those pleasures that's hard to describe if you haven't experienced it before. It's like having your own nest where, apart from your work tools, photographs, shirts, posters of some of the old glories of heroic cycling can all be accommodated. As time goes by, and as your passion becomes increasingly contagious, the workshop will be turned into a small artist's studio, a small museum, your own personal museum.

**The workshop**  Having a dedicated space arranged according to your own personal taste and needs so that it's comfortable and well-organized is the best way to devote yourself to your work with satisfaction. It takes time and money to set up such a space but with a little ingeniousnes and by doing it gradually you can contain the costs. Often, at the beginning, you make do, you're happy with a corner in the cellar, in the garage, sometimes out on the balcony... In other words, you find two square meters where you can feel free to do what you want. And to start out you really don't need much. A table and a sawhorse can suffice.

I set up my first workshop in the apartment where I was living, sacrificing the dining room. Then, as the number of restored bicycles grew, I started hanging them on the walls. Now I have more than thirty of them hanging here and there around the house. I'm sure this description will sound familiar to lots of you out there...

The workshop is a space where you spend a lot of time with yourself, but it's also where you welcome friends and fellow workers who are passing through. Days on end are spent there talking about everything, your hands dirty with grease, a glass of wine and... some good music playing in the background! Yes, one of the first things I do when I get to work is turn on the radio. Music is part and parcel of the work I do on bikes, maybe because they both give you that same feeling of freedom. On many days music is my only companion, mixed in with the sounds of the job I love, like the buzzing of the freewheel bearings as the wheel spins.

Another thing that's typical of every workshop is the smell. After a while that you've been working in your space, you'll become aware of the fact that it has its own particular smell, and when you can't smell it anymore it's the thing you'll miss the most.

I'm lucky to have my own space just below my house, but I can assure you the place where I really feel at home is... the workshop. I think that's because it's made to fit my skin, my pleasures, and my passions. Before starting any restoration or other project it's essential to find a space for yourself and organize it in the best way possible. Let's see how.

**Furnishings and supports**  Once you've found the right space for your activity, you need to fit it out with at least a few tools so that you can work more easily. To start with, all you need are a few simple furnishings, adding whatever you need for your restoration projects in the course of time.

First of all, you absolutely need a bike stand. There are various types and models on sale, so just choose the one that's best suited to your working method.

Second, you'll need a good workbench. Even an old wooden table can do the job; what's important is that it's stable. A used carpenter's or mechanic's bench is perfect, if you're lucky enough to find one.

Once you've taken care of the stand and the worktable, it's time to build a wall rack for the tools. A simple wooden panel with nails is sufficient: it's cheap but practical.

Lighting is also important, so if there isn't enough light in the place itself you'll need to get some good artificial lighting.

Another thing you won't want to overlook, especially if the space you've chosen to work in is cramped, is how it's organized, so you can move around comfortably. All it takes is a couple of dismantled bikes to fill a small space that's poorly organized. For this purpose exploit vertical space, both for the wheels and for whole bikes, by putting hooks on the wall. If the amount of space available is sufficient, I suggest leaving a part of one of the walls free where you can hang pictures of your restorations.

Above: After trying out a couple of them, I chose the stand in the picture. It's very stable and it allows me to work with both wheels assembled.

Below: Plastic containers of various sizes and seal top plastic bags for the smaller components help keep the workshop in order.

Opposite page: A table vise with aluminum supports to avoid ruining the metal parts, and a drill attached to the workbench, which comes in handy for lots of different jobs.

I always like to have my tools within easy reach, and plastic containers in various sizes or seal top plastic bags are useful for keeping all the small parts in order and for filing. You'll find lots of different models and sizes on sale, you'll be spoiled for choice. Personally, I use them a lot so I don't lose any pieces, especially the smallest ones, as well as to file them away after I've cleaned and polished them. You can use a felt-tip pen to write what the bags contain directly on them. This procedure, which might seem superfluous, is actually quite useful, both for learning the names of the various components, and also for forcing you to check and classify the specifics for each piece. Good filing also helps save space and time during the various restoration phases. Order is of essential importance for doing a good job.

To keep things tidy a bookcase or old pieces of furniture with drawers are also useful. I still remember when I came across a beautiful wooden cabinet that was once typically used in bike shops, with drawers of all sizes that had brass knobs. I realized instantly that it was the ideal piece of furniture for my workshop and I felt over the moon when I managed to buy it for next to nothing.

I get the same feeling of satisfaction when I think back to the day I bought my first table vise. I didn't feel like spending my money on a new one, I wanted something that was used, that had had a previous "life." It took several months to find one, but in the end mine was given to me by a very kind old man who lives nearby, and who is also crazy about bicycles. Along with the vise he also gave me a couple of light aluminum supports that I could apply to it to protect the metal parts.

The words of Ernesto Colnago often come to mind, recalled in the wonderful book by Rino Negri, *Quando la bici è arte* ("When a bicycle is a piece of art"): "How hard it was to furnish this workshop! His father gave him a mulberry wood table which he could use to make a workbench. The money he saved during his first years of racing he used to buy his first drill. Then came the vise. In Milan, in Corso Buenos Aires, Colnago bought screwdrivers and wrenches in various sizes." Yes, the drill: this is a key tool when you're restoring a bike. The drill is like your own personal electric arm: it speeds up some of the procedures and it's absolutely indispensable for others. It's used for paint stripping, sanding, and polishing. If you manage to find a table vise for the drill you can fasten it there and have it on hand for multiple purposes. To this regard, if you have the chance, consider creating a corner inside the workshop for all those jobs that produce lots of waste, like paint stripping, sanding, and polishing. I personally have set up a cubby hole for this purpose, which I have named "the magic room": parts or frames enter this room in terrible condition and they come out looking like jewels.

**Safety** While doing restoration work, besides organization, safety is of crucial importance. All you need to feel safe and protected is to follow a few basic rules. For your hands, you need a good pair of rubber gloves. Some products are harmful to the skin, while in other cases the gloves would allow you to get a better grip than if you were using your bare hands, especially when they've got grease on them. Remember that during all the restoration phases the "tools" that suffer most are your hands. Protect them, take care of them, and wash them with the right kind of soap. At the end of the day rub them with moisturizing

cream, especially if you have sensitive skin. When you're restoring a bike you're saving its life, just like a surgeon saves a person's life. This is why our hands are as important as those of a surgeon.

I suggest two types of goggles to protect the eyes, a simple one for small basic jobs, and one that's more like a mask and is used for dirtier jobs. When sanding, for instance, small sharp metal fragments can easily detach and fly off from the brushes.

As concerns breathing, besides making sure that the place you're working in has good air circulation, it's a good idea to wear a mask with interchangeable filters. Don't gamble on this aspect of the job! Some of the products you'll find yourself using are highly toxic and when stripping the paint or doing the polishing fine particles and vapors can be very harmful. Doing a good job also means protecting yourself carefully. The packaging for each of the products includes information concerning the degree of toxicity and the safety rules to be followed: it's important to read this information and to follow it 100%. Investing in three or four basic safety items is a priority. There's no point putting your health at risk. Restoration is a pleasure, keep that well in mind.

Anyone suffering from arthritis or similar ailments should always start out by doing exercises to loosen up the joints of the hands and fingers. More in general, everyone should do some simple stretching exercises: muscular warm-up exercises will help to avoid bothersome muscle strains or contractions in the parts of the body that are under the most pressure while doing the job.

**Products and tools used for cleaning**  As soon as you undertake a bike restoration you will need to use a wide range of cleaning products. There's a multitude of products with different brands available on the market, many of which serve the same purpose and are equally effective. I must confess, though, that many of them, at least to me, seem inefficient and/or too expensive, so I personally don't use many of them, at most a couple, maybe a few more. Given that a person's opinion on one product compared with another is always rather subjective, let's say that what's important is to be bold enough to experiment, testing the efficiency of each individual product and then choosing the best one. In time, trial and error has allowed me to find products that work better than the ones I used before, and consequently to improve the quality of the restoration itself. Special attention should be paid to the fact that some detergents are too aggressive and can harm the mechanical parts or the frame. Better to count on elbow grease than resort to products that might irreparably ruin the aesthetics of the relic we are holding in our hands.

There are products for general cleaning, lubrication and greasing, polishing, and paint stripping; there are protective oils and anti-corrosive and anti-rust substances. To clean the frame, I mostly use a polish and a spray that revives the paint. Usually I prefer products suited to the various metal alloys or in general to mechanical components, not necessarily specifically for bicycles.

For the saddles, I use only two products: a milk moisturizing cream and grease, both specifically suited to leather.

For a general cleaning, neutral soap and water can suffice. A brush dipped in diesel oil or gas can degrease even the the most encrusted parts. If you're on a shoestring budget, I suggest not spending money on expensive products, especially when there is a more affordable and equally effective range of products. If you manage to find some old tubes of grease don't let them get away: some of the older products are of unbeatable quality compared with what's available these days.

Often, you end up preferring one product over another. I have a list of a few items that I find irreplaceable. I use the lubricant WD40 and the degreaser Metarex particularly often. I don't how I'd manage without them. For other products, especially grease and lubricants for the components, I still try new things as I search for something that is completely to my satisfaction. Whatever the case may be, follow this rule of thumb: when you're about to use a product for

the first time, read the contents list carefully and the instructions for use, to make sure it's not going to damage the work you're about to do, as well as for safety reasons.

Besides the dedicated products, to clean your bike you need more generic items as well. Firstly, paper, which has myriad uses and is a must in the workshop. The same goes for the hand-cleansing paste. Also essential, as we said before, are gloves. Disposable latex gloves are ideal for polishing and painting; rubber gloves are used to handle toxic products and as a protection, especially when assembling and dismantling the components. I use white cotton gloves for putting the finishing touches, such as the final polishing phase or applying the decals.

In addition to the ones used for basic cleaning, lots of highly particular products are used for restoration. For the rust on the surface, as well as grease or oxidation, different types of brushes will be useful, with bristles made of plastic, brass, or iron. For the sanding phase the choice of brushes is also vast, and brushes can be attached to the drill if necessary, whereas to remove both paint and the toughest rust various types of sand paper are available on the market.

This equipment is relatively inexpensive, but generally very useful, especially for the harder jobs where elbow grease is not enough. As previously stated, the opinion on the effectiveness of these utensils is subjective and can vary over time. I myself had to wait months to try lots of them before I found what I was looking for, and whenever I find a brush or a disk that's better than the ones I routinely use I don't hesitate to adopt them. Sometimes you'll make a mistake, but it's nothing to worry about. And don't hesitate to learn from those who have your same passion, watching what they do and asking for advice. Even today I

consult with friends for a continuous constructive exchange of opinions on the trade.

One tool that's essential when you're doing this kind of work is an air compressor. In addition to allowing you to pump the wheels or tubulars at the right pressure, it can come in very handy for cleaning and drying as well. To remove dirt, grease, and rust, sandpaper with different grits is used, along with steel wool, sponges, and glass wool. Paintbrushes can also be very useful for

My favourite polishing kit: it contains four fabric disks and four matching pastes. Disk and paste A is used at the beginning to eliminate the oxidation; then I move on to disk and paste B, followed by disk C and its corresponding paste to finish off the polishing. I use disk and paste Z instead of the A combination when the oxidation is more widespread and deeper.

certain procedures: they can be used to remove dust or, after dipping them in a solvent or diesel oil, to dissolve any stubborn grease. To clean the tires, especially the light colored ones or the canvas part of the tubulars, I often use a brush with plastic bristles soaked in water and neutral soap or degreasing liquid. Other tools that can turn out to be useful in many situations are adhesive tape of various kinds and colors, masking tape, and cutters. Except for the compressor, which might take a hefty chunk out of your budget, the rest of these products are inexpensive and, as I said before, you may already have a few of them around the house.

Curiosity about experimenting with new materials is at the heart of a job well done. Discovering better products, ones that might be more effective or good enough to make the job run more smoothly, is exciting. Along these lines I like to remember the time I discovered the abrasive paste and disks that I normally use to polish metal. I saw it for the first time online, but not being able to actually see whether it worked, I put off buying it. Later, while visiting a vintage motorcycle and

bicycle trade fair, I had the chance to try one out and I was amazed by how strong it was and how easy it was to use. I bought two of them, along with a vise for drills. I've lost track of all the pastes and disks I've used up since them! It's one of those products I can't do without: the protection it provides against oxidation is unequalled, as is its efficiency when you have to bring one of the components back to life.

As a rule, with disks you go from using the hardest to the softest. Using disks to clean and polish requires some skill, especially in using the grindstone; before using it it's best to find out how it works and get some practice. There are some great videos that can easily be found online. Once you've learned to use these tools correctly the quality of your restoration work will greatly improve and you'll get the job done in half as much time. Now that we've discussed the products and materials you will find yourself using during the cleaning phase at length, let's examine the tools required to assemble and dismantle the pieces. I have divided them into two large groups: basic tools and ones specifically used for bicycles.

# AN ICON OF HEROIC CYCLING

*Luciano Berruti*

—

An icon on today's heroic cycling scene and the founder of the Cosseria Bicycle Museum

I've always loved the outdoor life, in contact with nature, maybe because I was brought up in a small town in the countryside. My desire for freedom and movement stood out even when I was a child. I was very lively—I was often sent marching off to the corner of the classroom at school because I couldn't keep still—I liked to climb trees and I enjoyed drawing and building all sorts of objects. And I also liked bicycles.

From when I was a child I was fascinated by the figure of Lucien Petit-Breton, winner of two Tours de France, a Milan-Sanremo, and a Paris-Tours in the early twentieth century. The story of his life was amazing. He was extremely enterprising and always avant-garde, a technician always hunting for new solutions. He even went so far as to lose a Giro d'Italia due to a breakdown in his prototype gears. On that occasion, he wrote a letter of apology specifying that the bike (he was racing for Fiat at the time) was perfect, and that the breaking of the hub had been solely his fault. He also made an attempt to break the one-hour record, but his career came to a premature halt when the First World War broke out, during which he allegedly died from the consequences of an accident involving military vehicles.

On the back of this passion, when I was very young I started cycling myself: road bike, mountain bike, cyclo-cross. Competition, a few victories—but also too many accidents which forced me on the sidelines for lengthy periods of time—until around the mid-1990s, when I discovered my passion for heroic cycling.

One day I showed up at an uphill time trial that was being held near my town with an old Paris-Roubaix Bianchi model from the 1950s. I wanted to show that it's men that make the difference, not bikes. It was fun. I came in second because at the point where the hill ended and a flat stretch began I was unable to change gears and launch my attack. Back then, I wasn't so good at certain techniques. I also showed up with the same bike at a line race, but the judges wouldn't even let me get started because they felt that by riding that bike I was making fun of the other competitors. I swear, that wasn't my intention!

A while later I found out that in Tuscany a race was going to be held for vintage bikes on dirt roads: it was the Eroica. It was love at first sight, it overwhelmed me and left me powerless to resist, and that love continues to this day.

Driven by the same passion I started collecting and restoring bikes and period materials, including riding gear and other accessories. After being invited several times to exhibit some of these relics during events or bicycle races, always with great success among both enthusiasts and curiosity-seekers, little by little I started thinking about opening a permanent museum in my native town. So, thanks to the town's administration and that of the Region, I was able to find the venue and the funding that led to the creation of the Museo della Bicicletta (www.veloretro.it) in Cosseria.

I would like my example to infect young people in particular. To those who truly want to "taste" the essence of heroic cycling I say: get yourself an old bike with its original gears, do miles and miles without support and without assistance, eating and drinking whatever you come across along the way. This is what the pioneers of cycling used to do, this was perfectly normal for them. Only by trying all this out in person can you really understand what the cycling of the "heroes" of times past really was like.

**Basic equipment** A passion for vintage bikes and their restoration can lead to developing a passion for the world of period cycling as a whole, and you can even end up falling in love not just with the bicycles but also with the individual components or the clothing, and even the tools used to do the job.

Over the years I've had the chance to meet many historical cycling enthusiasts and many of them were exclusively in search of the tools. And not because they needed them for their work, but just for the pleasure of collecting them. I remember a retired mechanic who had transferred his workshop, by then closed to the public, to his home garage, and continued to do small repair jobs for the townspeople. When I went to see him looking for some parts I needed, I was amazed to see how much equipment he had. He especially loved threading tools and had special crates filled with tools for bicycles of a variety of Italian and foreign brands. He had numerous wooden boxes filled with tools and a workbench that was super-equipped. He had even built a mechanical arm that served as a stand and that he controlled via a junction box as if it were a robot. I was amazed by that contraption, the fruit of Italian genius; he never missed a chance to show me some box of tools he'd just found, explaining proudly how each individual component was used. That day I realized just how much beauty can lie within an object that may appear to be ordinary, such as a wrench or a hammer.

But let's go back to our theme. Needless to say, the first time you approach restoration you can't expect to have every possible tool on hand right away, but you will have to find the ones that are absolutely necessary in order to carry out the basic operations of dismantling and reassembling. Like the material and the products I discussed previously, it is likely that many of the general tools described below are already lying around your home. Ordinary DIY toolboxes usually contain a good range.

Four categories of tools that you'll be using all the time are a complete set of hammers, files of various types and sizes, two gauges for precision measurements, and two measuring sticks, one in inches (yardstick) and the other in centimeters (meter); lastly, you're going to need a complete set of screwdrivers. These are common tools and before going out to buy them make sure you don't already have them at home. You won't need five hammers or twenty screwdrivers; a couple of elements for each of these categories is more than enough to get started.

There's no need to hurry. I can assure you that completing your workshop with the tools you need as you need them is in itself very satisfying, a real pleasure.

If you're not really into DIY and you don't have much at all in the way of tools, before spending money go see a friend or a family member. As far as I'm concerned, at the beginning I could count on the kindness and generosity of my father, who gave me all the tools he no longer needed but that for me were very important. I also suggest visiting the various antiques and used goods markets where you can often find whole sets on sale for next to nothing, and where you can get a bargain.

Buying brand new tools can be economically taxing, especially if they're of good quality. If you have the chance to buy them used, make sure they're in working condition. And always remember that a good-quality tool has a higher price tag attached. Sometimes I come upon sets with three hundred tools at very low prices. If you divide the price of the set by the number of tools it contains the single tool will cost just a few cents. It's fairly obvious that a tool that costs just a few cents can't be made well. So steer away from those super-cheap multisets because they're not going to be high quality. Better to own a few tools less but all of them well-made.

Remember that, like your bike, your tools also need care and maintenance. You should clean them regularly, let's say once a month, removing grease and dirt and making sure they're not worn. This will help to avoid damaging any threads or hurting yourself if they're oily and greasy while you're handling them. Cleaning your tools also gives you the opportunity to arrange them properly inside the workshop. Your restoration work will benefit from working in an environment that's clean and organized.

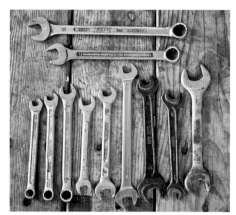

Another category of basic tools you won't be able to do without are hex keys of various sizes, possibly also with different grips. To this regard it may be useful to know that in some countries like the United States this type of tool also comes in half-sizes; in Europe, on the contrary, whole sizes are almost always used (e.g. seven millimeters, eight millimeters, etc.). But not always... I remember, for example, that Campagnolo, for the Delta brake cable retainer, differed from the Italian standard of four millimeters by using four and a half millimeters.

Also indispensable are pliers, wrenches, and cutters. I should stress the importance of having a good cable-cutter and good needle nose pliers, both of which are used frequently, just as you're going to need classic flat wrenches in various sizes (for bicycles you won't need a complete set, wrenches from 7 to 17 millimeters will be sufficient) and a series of hex wrenches (the ones used for bicycles generally measure from 7 to 14 millimeters).

**Specific tools** Let's now take a look at the second category of tools, the ones that are specifically used for bikes. It's a vast world and the one I'm presenting here is my own personal selection, indicative of the ones that are used the most and are the most useful, as well as essential. I wouldn't dismantle or assemble a piece that requires a specific tool instead of trying to make do with a general one that's not suited because there's a high risk of undermining the outcome of the work, irreparably damaging pieces or threading.

Another important premise for those who aren't familiar with tools like these is to be informed before handling them. Some of them can be easy to use if you follow your instinct, but others require special skills. If you have a friend who's an expert or a mechanic near where you live, try asking them for information. You can also find good support online among the various groups and forums dedicated to bicycle maintenance. Turning to expert hands will mean avoiding having to pay for the consequences of a job poorly done. Don't look at it as a personal affront: even skilled restorers need to get help from others. I often need to as well and I think it makes sense, if there's someone who knows how to do a job better than you, to turn to them for help, because it will benefit the final quality of the restoration.

Available on the market are lots of sets of tools, ranging from beginner to advanced to professional, and for those interested in this world buying one of them can be a good starting point. Also extremely useful, if you have the good fortune of finding one at a market or at a trade show, are period sets, a real godsend for restorers and very much sought after by collectors. Unfortunately, they're usually rather expensive.

Wrench set for the Campagnolo bicycle.

Opposite: Two chain breakers, one for 1/8 chains, the other for 3/32 chains.

Below: Flat wrenches for the hub washers (left), and extractors, wrenches and specific tools used to disassemble the cottered crank and the cotterless crank (right).

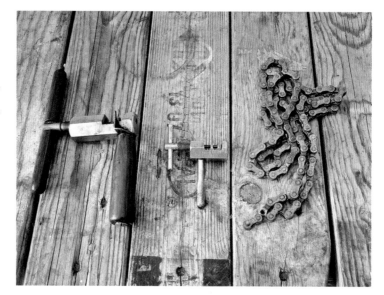

You can't do without a chain breaker of excellent quality and a series of cone wrenches specifically for hub cones and counter-cones, usually in pairs of 13/14 and 15/16 millimeters. Equally important are the tools used to dismantle the crank arms, both cottered cranks and square taper cranks. The former should be used with various types of steel awls.

Other multipurpose wrenches that are required for various dismantling and assembling procedures can be found in the bag under the saddle. Although the quality is generally average, they can still be useful because they're often of a specific size that's hard to find elsewhere. If you happen to run across some of these, hold on to them

because they'll come in handy on many occasions.

Another specific group of tools is the one used to dismantle and assemble the headset. These tools are used for most threaded headset models in bicycles manufactured before the 1990s. Some models, however—for example the headset in the Shimano 600 group or certain Mavic models from the 1980s—have a clamping bolt that requires a special wrench. What to do when you don't have one is discussed in the following chapter, which analyzes each component in depth. Sometimes you simply don't have the proper tool to dismantle or reassemble a piece. When that is the case other methods can be used, all you need to do is think hard and

Some of the wrenches typically found in the set in the bag under the saddle. Note in particular the two wrenches used to dismantle the saddle, with a typical "step" shape that makes the procedure easier.

Set of tools used to dismantle and assemble the headset. The long tool at the top is used to assemble the headset race cups to be inserted in the frame, while to dismantle them you need to use the black tube-shaped tool that spreads out like a fan at the end. Needle nose pliers can be used for the clamping bolts with knurling that are often hard to remove by hand. The other two tools next to the hammer can be used for the same purpose, screwing and unscrewing the clamping bolts featuring small holes (this is often found, for example, in the 1950s Bianchi headset as well as in other models). The two pliers are not specific for this procedure, but they still do the job. Then there's the usual cone wrenches, normally 32 millimeters in size. The two U-shaped tools next to them are used to extract the fork crown race. To put the same cup back on the fork you need to use a tool with a cylindrical shape.

Tools used to assemble and dismantle the bottom bracket. At the center the same wrenches used for the headset, but used here with a different function. The toothed part is used to loosen and tighten the lock ring of the bottom bracket. The photograph shows three types, with different cogs, suited to different types of rings. Some rings are simply knurled and require the use of needle nose pliers. Again, to screw and regulate the left cup we can use the wrenches at the bottom of the picture. The two awls on the far right fit like pivots into the bore-holes present in the left cup of the bottom bracket. Notice that the darker of the two in the picture has an arm that can be regulated so that it fits several models of cups. After unscrewing the lock ring, usually the left adjustable race can be removed by hand or with a specific double pin spanner. If the cup is encrusted and hard to remove, a more specific spanner can be used, the fourth one from the left in the picture. That type of spanner has various pins that (depending on the model) are able to grab all six holes of the adjustable cup and can be screwed to it. Should more force be required to unscrew the cup both hands can be used. Different tools are used for the left cup which is usually harder to remove. Although in some cases specific wrenches are available depending on the model and the brand, for the most common vintage bottom brackets the two tools to the left in the picture are used. The third wrench is used for the same purpose, but it's more specific to certain brands and types. For more modern models, let's say manufactured after the 1980s, specific tools such as the three wrenches on the right are needed.

try out what you come up with. Furthermore, as you may have noticed in this series of specific tools for the headset, the same piece often requires two different tools for assembling and dismantling.

I should add that you won't necessarily always have to dismantle the entire headset. For conservative restoration, for instance, unless some particular problem comes up, the headset will only need to be cleaned and greased. This means that only the lock nut will have to be taken apart, without needing to remove the races from the frame. All you'll need to do this is a thin wrench and needle nose pliers.

Just like the headset, the bottom bracket also has a series of dedicated tools.

What we said before applies here as well: not every tool will be needed from the very beginning. When I started doing this job, all I had were a couple of the wrenches in the picture, and only as time went by did I acquire all the others. To get started, two wrenches and needle nose pliers are sufficient. Note that the bottom bracket is the heart, the very core of the bicycle. This part of the bike is very sensitive to environmental conditions and to rain, and the lug containing

it is crucially important. Obtaining the tools required for its maintenance is essential for the restoration of this mechanical part.

As for the wrenches used for the pedals, their specific tools were mostly supplied with the pedals themselves.

Each pedal has its own type of cap and its specific wrench, and rarely are the models similar enough to allow you to use the same keys. Note, however, that regardless of the model, the dust caps can be dismantled by using simple needle nose pliers, and with the help of a vise, you can also take apart the axle. Obviously, specialized wrenches make the work easier. From experience, I can safely say that investing in a professional wrench to assemble and dismantle the pedals is a necessary step. As concerns the tools used for

the maintenance of the pedals, there are many efficient ones to choose from.

The wheels—made up of spokes, rims, tires, or tubulars—also have a series of dedicated tools.

Remember: the wheels are an aesthetically important part of the bicycle. The visual impact of a pair of state-of-the-art restored wheels is great. This is something that should be kept in mind when you're deciding to replace some piece or leave some time-worn ones.

If possible, it's best to preserve all the parts of the original wheel, limiting yourself to cleaning and polishing them, an activity that's very simple if you've taken them apart one by one. The task may be long and complex, but the final results are no doubt better. Furthermore, this way we have the chance to understand how a wheel is laced,

This picture shows my personal evolution in getting the tools I needed to assemble and dismantle the pedals. At the outset, I had managed to get a basic set that included the pair of black wrenches. They were low quality tools and were almost immediately ruined. In addition, they have a small grip that's not very functional. Later, I got myself a similar wrench, the one with the blue handle, which did its job perfectly for a good long time. Unfortunately, the quality of the metal wasn't the best and with prolonged use it was pretty much ruined. That was when I went looking for a professional wrench (the one that's completely made of metal to the left of it) and I finally found a tool that still satisfies me today. It's made of a very resilient alloy, and after two years of use it's still going strong. The grip is excellent and it guarantees a secure hold. To the far right you can see an older cone wrench, on which you can read the size of the standard thread: 9/16 x 20 tpi. Different types of thread can be found in the various groups. Lastly, small wrenches are used specifically for pedal maintenance: double wrenches are used to remove the dust caps that protect the pedal axle, and to open the bolt that adjusts the axle. In the meantime, the third wrench is used to block the axle during this procedure.

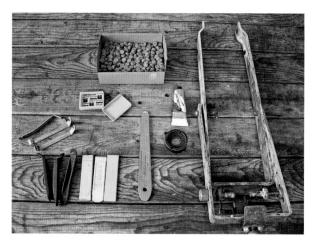

Tools required for the wheels. The largest tool in the picture is a wheel truing stand, and the same is used in combination with the small circular spoke wrench on the left. Both are indispensable for building and maintaining the wheels. To take care of and repair the tubulars or the air chambers in the tires a kit with specific pieces and glue will come in handy. To assemble the tubulars you need special glue or mastic (the tube on the left in the picture). For more refined, attentive restorers I've added to the photograph several small cork caps (the ones in the cardboard box): at one time they were used to close the spoke holes on the rim. This way the glue used to fasten the tubular wouldn't come out, and at the same time it prevented any water getting in from the outside. It also created a more homogeneous surface on which to spread the mastic so that the tubular had a more uniform hold in the rim. This apparently banal accessory which is actually of great use is really hard to find; luckily, it can easily be reproduced. Pictured at the bottom of the photograph are three different groups of tools with the same function referred to in jargon as tire levers. I've added three different types to stress the importance of having a good tool: for some tires plastic or aluminum levers won't do because they can easily bend and break. The larger lever on the right is a professional one and practically impossible to destroy.

In the picture, I have grouped together a multitude of extractors necessary to remove the freewheel. Generally, they came with the freewheel, since every brand and model had its own extractor. Another tool that's used to take the freewheel apart is the chain whip, to the right in the picture.

when the time comes to put it back on. Lacing is an operation that requires a great deal of experience and skill. I personally consider it an art and still prefer to have a professional do the job.

The last specific set of tools to examine is the one that's used to remove the freewheel. I have to admit that this is a type of tool that is often overlooked, but with time you learn to appreciate its usefulness. It's also hard to find, maybe because being so small it's easy to lose it in the multitude of tools in a workshop. Arm yourself with patience, and try to at least find the ones made by and for the major brands. In the past, as well, the existence of many different models was often a headache for mechanics, and I've often come across home-made tools that were meant to solve the problem. Toward the mid-1980s the situation

improved considerably, when manufacturers gradually adopted standards for the production of this specific component. Consequently, the variety of wrenches used to remove it has also diminished.

As an alternative, a tool widely used to dismantle and assemble the freewheel is the simple chain whip. No doubt the universal one should be used, but sometimes it requires considerable effort. That's why specific extractors are simpler and more effective to use.

In conclusion, we've outlined all the products, materials, and tools needed to set up a good workshop and that will be of use during the various phases of the restoration, whether conservative, total, or creative. Once we've completed our space with these tools we will finally be ready to... get our hands dirty.

# CONSERVATIVE RESTORATION

---

4

L et me start out by saying this: many of the procedures that we will examine in this chapter dedicated to conservative restoration are also suited to the total or creative restoration that is discussed in the next chapter. But not just that: some of the procedures described here also come in handy for basic bicycle maintenance. Procedures like cleaning, greasing, and restoring mechanical function are indispensable for the proper functioning of the bicycle regardless of the restoration process.

**Photographic chart and informative notes**  Besides bicycles I have another great passion, which is photography, and very often the two go hand in hand. Photography is an indispensable tool in the various restoration phases. From beginning to end, photos serve as a form of documentation and recording, either to be able to appreciate the work done, or as a point of reference, for example, when you need to make sure you're reassembling the components correctly. And, needless to say, photographs are also the most efficient way to share your work on the various social networks... It is certainly much simpler to take pictures today than it was in the past. You don't need professional equipment, all you need is a smartphone to get excellent results.

From the very beginning, when maybe you're still trying to decide whether or not to buy a certain bike to restore, if you take pictures you can show them to a friend or to someone at work, who can help you make a decision. Sometimes words aren't enough to describe what something looks like.

As a rule, when I have a bicycle to restore I start by taking a series of descriptive photographs. This gives me an accurate idea of the general conditions at the time of my "discovery." I try to highlight all the parts that need to be restored: the frame, the mechanical parts, the wheels. I usually take about fifty pictures at the beginning, and I take just as many when I've finished restoring the bike. During all the intermediate phases, for example, when I'm cleaning the pieces, sometimes I need to dismantle one into its individu-

al components, so having a photograph will be helpful when I have to put it back together in the right order.

When you've done your fair share of restorations, a photo archive will help you to memorize the frames, components, and details of each individual bicycle, but also to improve your work. Furthermore, by keeping a photo archive you'll be contributing to the historical documentation overall, which would otherwise be lost. Sharing the photos of a complete restoration offers others the opportunity to be informed, and allows you to use your own work as a reference. If you used the Internet when you first started getting into this type of work, then it's ethically correct to share your experience on the Web once you've completed your work.

In other words, a camera or a smartphone should be considered an indispensable "tool" for the restoration process.

In addition to the descriptive photos, at the beginning it will be useful to write up a fact sheet about the bicycle. Besides the brand, model, and measurements, you should jot down any serious problems you've run into, making a list of the parts that need to be replaced or that are missing, and the various jobs that need to be done. Personally, I never start a project if I'm not sure I'm going to find the right components to complete it. Especially when you're conservatively restoring bicycles that were manufactured in the 1930s or '40s, or ones that are even older, it's often hard to find the original parts, as well as being costly. Making a list of the problems you're going to have to deal with and the parts you're going to have to find will give you a clear idea of the time frame and the costs you can expect, and help you to organize your work more efficiently.

To complete the written description with all the facts concerning the bike I use old catalogues and period trade magazines. You can find a lot of information on the Internet, both in the company websites and in the countless forums and groups dedicated to vintage bike restoration. Particularly if you're a rookie, consult those who have had more experience. Collecting lots of information—from different sources—will add to your knowledge and certify its accuracy. Let's ad-

Several photographs of a bicycle
taken at the beginning of this
restoration project.

mit it: maybe without the Internet and the social networks there might not have been such a boom in vintage bike enthusiasts. Without the Internet, it would have been impossible to complete many of the restorations because of problems finding the components, which are closely linked to the area where they were produced and sold. In the old days, all you had were markets, trade fairs, or specialized exchange exhibitions. Today everything is much more accessible, although there can be some confusion at times...

Besides magazines, old catalogues, and the Web, there are lots of bicycle books on the market. Sometimes before getting your hands dirty, it's worth it to tire your eyes with a good read.

**Dismantling the components**  Whenever I take a bike apart I always follow a specific sequence, the one that seems the most logical to me. This is my personal approach, however, so feel free to follow the order you prefer. I should say two things, though. First of all, while some actions are easy and intuitive, others are more complicated and,

especially if you're doing them for the first time and you don't feel confident, don't hesitate to ask for help. Second, even if, depending on the conditions of the bike, some parts don't need to be taken apart and cleaned, theoretically speaking, I personally tend to dismantle everything. That way I'll be sure to check each individual component.

The first thing to do is prepare a plastic container in which to collect all the dismantled parts; seal top plastic bags can be used for the smaller parts, like bolts, nuts, and bearings. Furthermore, before starting you should moisten each screw and thread of the bicycle parts with multipurpose lubricant and let it do its work for a few minutes. This will help when you're disassembling the parts, especially if there's rust and oxidation. For some parts that are especially sensitive, like the seatpost, the stem, and the pedals, lots of lubricant should be used.

Let's take the wheels apart and mount the frame in a bike stand or a similar support.

After waiting for the lubricant to do its work, use a pair of pliers to cut the cables of

the two brakes and the derailleurs, if present, and remove them from the housings. You'll need the right tool to unravel the chain. Some chains are closed with a double link system, in which case you won't need a specific extractor; a pair of pliers or a screwdriver will do. Then let's disassemble the various parts, from the seatpost to the saddle, and last of all the bottom bracket. Until the 1950s, most seatposts were made from iron, but since then they have generally been made from aluminum. If the bicycle hasn't been taken care of on a regular basis, whether the seatpost is made of iron or aluminum, the oxidation will still be hard to remove.

Depending on the bicycle itself and the year it was produced, you'll run into various types of closing binder bolts for the seatpost (inside socket or outside hex bolt). After loosening the binder bolt, with the help of the saddle pull out the seatpost. If there isn't a lot of rust or oxidation it shouldn't take long. At this point, you can remove the saddle from the seatpost. There are lots of saddle models available, and an equally large number of saddle clamps, some of which require the use of special wrenches.

If the seatpost won't budge either sideways or upwards, then the problem is serious and there are different ways to solve it. Let's start with the least invasive one. Allow me to say first that this operation is best carried out when the bicycle is completely dismantled, so that you can work on and have access to the bottom bracket shell. In fact, once you've removed the bottom bracket you can turn the bike upside down and let the lubricant inside the seatpost tube drip down, and thus more effectively reach the part of the seatpost that's oxidated inside the tube. I suggest using lots of lubricant and giving it time to work, meaning at least twelve hours. The frame should be kept in the same upside down position.

If this is still not enough to solve the problem, then you'll have to be more aggressive: remove the saddle leaving only the seatpost inserted in the frame and, with the bicycle in an upside down position, use a vise to block it together with the frame, making sure you use alu-

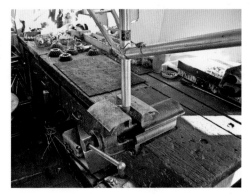

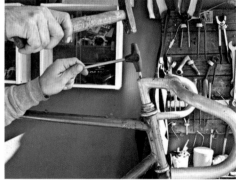

minum supports for the vise to avoid ruining it. Now, careful not to break the seatpost or damage the frame, use both hands to push down on the frame. Move it side to side and then pull up to extract the frame.

If you still can't get the seatpost loose, try using the kind of dryer that's used in body shops. Metal expands when it's heated, and this can come in handy in certain situations. Warm the seatpost tube and the seatpost lug where the seatpost is inserted until it gets almost too hot to touch, so as to avoid ruining the paint, and then try to unblock the seatpost by moving it from side to side. Usually, with patience and a little elbow grease, you'll finally be able to extract it. Only a couple of times in my experience have I ended up breaking it inside the tube. Unfortunately, when you're restoring a bike you have to be ready for this kind of drawback to occur as well.

Now it's time to extract the stem from the frame, with the handlebar and the levers still mounted. In this case too, there are mainly two types of closings: inside long socket or outside long hex bolt. After loosening the bolt, check to see if the handlebar is loose and ready to be removed. In the former case, lightly hammer the socket or the hex bolt to make the expander or the wedge come down; that way it won't block the stem and you'll be able to remove it. If the handlebar won't budge, then turn the frame upside down and lubricate the inside of the fork from the hole underneath. Let the lubricant do its work and then repeat.

Once the handlebar has been removed, proceed by removing the handlebar tape and brake levers. Again, depending on the model and the year the bike was manufactured, there are different types of closings, sockets or screw bolts, and closings with a hex bolt are also very common. Once you've loosened up or unscrewed the bolt a bit, extract the lever with the closing ring still partially attached. If instead you don't want to replace the tape, completely unscrew the lever leaving the closing ring inserted in the handlebar.

After you've removed the brake levers, proceed to free the stem from the handlebar. Here again, vintage bikes usually have two types of quill stem closings: the usual hex bolt or the socket type.

The tools needed to carry out the various jobs described up to this point are rather common ones and, unless something particular comes up, everything should run smoothly. The same goes for the disassembling of the brake calipers, the

pedals, the gear unit and any accessories such as fenders, chainguards, lights and dynamos. This mostly involves unscrewing some screws and bolts. Since these are the parts that are most exposed to atmospheric agents, you might find that some of the bolts are very rusty, or partially stripped and ruined. Should that be the case carefully remove any dirt and rust first.

If the bicycle you're restoring has gears, then disassemble the rear and front derailleurs and the shifting levers. These are all straightforward, common sense operations. To dismantle the brake calipers, both the front and the rear ones, you should, again depending on the model and the year or the type of bicycle, unscrew the traditional hex nut or the usual recessed nut, and then remove the calipers from the frame.

Now it's time to remove the pedals, which often turns out to be a real challenge. The lubricant applied at the beginning should have solved any problems related to rust or oxidation. You're

going to need to get a good grip on them so be sure to use a high-quality wrench. Because of the strength you'll need to exert to do the job properly, a poor-quality wrench might break. Remember that the right-hand side pedal is loosened by turning the wrench counterclockwise, like a normal screw, while the one on the left-hand side has to be turned clockwise.

Let's move on to the crank arms. Unlike the procedures seen so far, for the crank arms you'll need a specific extractor. Furthermore, for this component there have been various updates over the years: until the 1960s, the most common model was the cottered crank; it was later replaced by the square taped "cotterless" type. These are the two types you come across most often when restoring bikes. The construction material has changed as well, from iron, used until the late 1950s, to aluminum, which is lighter. Square taped cranks are locked with a hex bolt screwed directly onto the axle of the bottom bracket, which is normally covered by a protective dust cap. Cap models vary depending on the brand, the main differences being the material used and the closing. The latter can be of the socket screw, two-hole, or buttonhole type. Buttonhole closings can simply be unscrewed with a coin, while a specific wrench is used for two-hole closings; if you don't have a wrench, use two nails or the tip of a small pair of pliers. Once you've removed the two caps from the crank arm, unscrew the bolt from the right crank arm, using the proper wrench or a simple tubular one, and then unscrew the same bolt on the left crank arm.

Having removed the bolts, proceed to remove the crank arms using the proper extractor, and once you've removed them, dismantle the chainrings from the right arm. It should be enough to unscrew the binder bolts, but sometimes they spin freely. When that happens you can use the same tool you used before for the caps with the micro holes, which has a twofold function and serves to block the female part of the binder bolt.

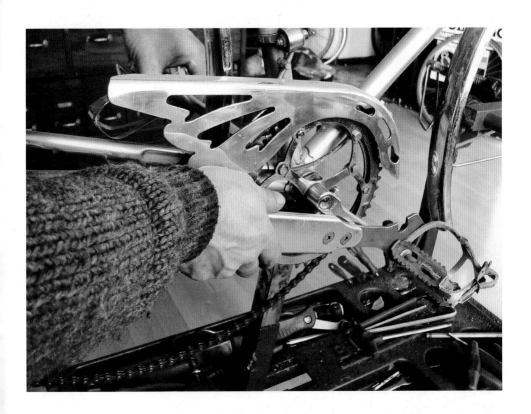

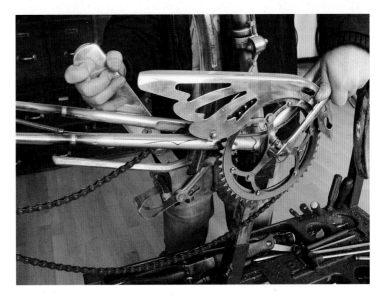

For cottered crank arms continue by loosening the nut without unscrewing it completely. I suggest soaking it in lubricant and letting it rest for a few minutes. Afterwards, use a hammer and an awl to strike the nut and remove it from the cottered crank, then unscrew the nut completely so that it comes out of the crank arm. Leaving the bolt still screwed prevents damaging the thread during hammering. This is a procedure that causes problems at times, and requires a certain amount of strength, but with enough lubricant you usually succeed. Unfortunately, quite often, due to the strength needed to hammer, some nuts get damaged and have to be replaced.

After the crank arm has been removed, it's time to disassemble the headset and the bottom bracket, two of the most complicated procedures of all, especially if you don't have the proper tools.

As concerns the headset, something needs to be said first. In conservative restoration you're not forced to dismantle it completely. To evaluate its conditions, all you need to do is unscrew the lock nut and the adjustable race (if you're not familiar

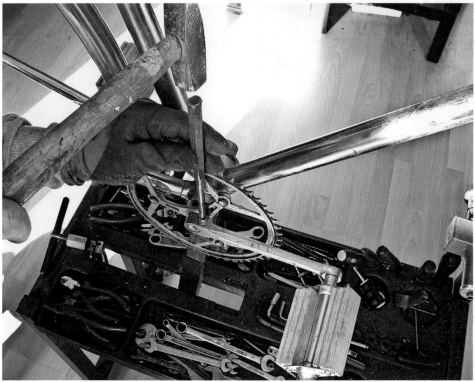

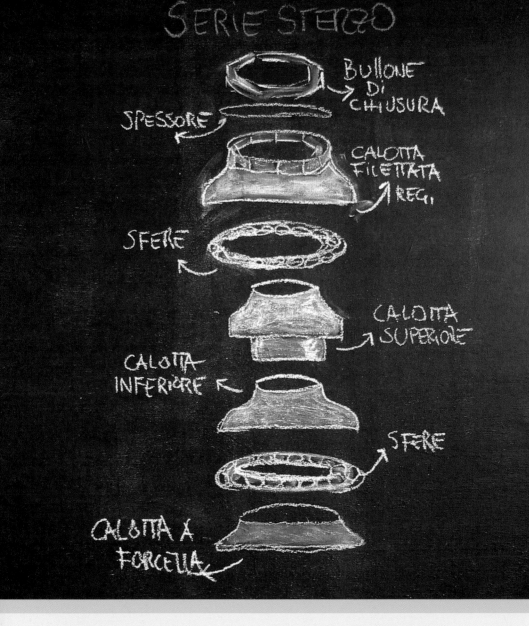

SERIE STERZO

- BULLONE DI CHIUSURA
- SPESSORE
- CALOTTA FILETTATA REG.
- SFERE
- CALOTTA SUPERIORE
- CALOTTA INFERIORE
- SFERE
- CALOTTA A FORCELLA

HEADSET
(Clockwise from the top)

– LOCK NUT
– TOP ADJUSTABLE RACE
– TOP SET RACE
– BEARINGS
– FORK CROWN RACE
– BOTTOM SET RACE
– BEARINGS
– SPACER

with this component, refer to the blackboard) and only if, after careful inspection, you notice that the inside of the races is worn and needs to be replaced should you proceed with complete disassembly (this is further discussed in Chapter Six). It's also useful to know that the headset is stressed both by the rotation of the wheels and by the vibrations and recoil coming from the fork.

Having said this, continue with the dismantling. Use a wrench to unscrew the lock nut and then do the same to the adjustable race. Needless to say, once again there are several types and models; in this specific case, we're referring to a pre-1960s bike model. Here the adjustable race is knurled and can usually be unscrewed quite easily with your bare hands; otherwise use a pair of nose pliers. There may be a washer between the lock nut and the adjustable race; this can be easily removed. Once you've unscrewed the lock nut and removed the washer and the race, extract

the fork and check the state of all the relevant parts. At this point you'll come across the bearings, which might be inside a cage or, especially in pre-1960s models, free to move around. Keep a magnet on hand to prevent the bearings from rolling around everywhere.

If you don't succeed in unscrewing the adjustable race with a pair of nose pliers, then you can try a more aggressive method: turn the frame upside down and fasten the race to the vise (don't forget to use aluminum supports so it doesn't get ruined). Find a piece of wood or a hard plastic tube and insert it in the fork. Use it as a lever as you try to get a rotating movement going. Since there are many models and types of headsets, you often find you don't have the proper wrench, and this method, although rather invasive, can help solve the problem.

Now you have access to all the parts of the headset, so you can check for any signs of wear and tear in the surfaces where the bearings move, and clean and grease them. If necessary, they can also be replaced.

Now let's move on to the bottom bracket, the basic part of a bicycle's mechanism. Just as you did for the headset, you'll need to evaluate, clean, and re-grease all the parts. This should be done using the proper tools. As usual, if you're inexperienced, get a specialized mechanic to do the job. Incorrect disassembling and reassembling can lead to a series of unforeseen consequences and damage that are best avoided. What we said earlier also applies to the different models and types of bottom bracket. Usually the ones that can be submitted to careful maintenance are the ones featuring bearings or caged bearings, not the ones with sealed bearings or a sealed cartridge.

Start by dismantling the lock ring on the adjusting cup. Using a lock ring wrench will make the procedure easy, but if you don't have one then use nose pliers again. Once you've removed the ring, use the proper wrench to unscrew the adjusting cup, possibly after lubricating the exposed thread to make things easier. Then extract the axle, the sleeve if there is one, and the bearings, again using a magnet to keep them in one place. At this point only the fixed cup will need to be dismantled. Before proceeding, lubricate the part well again, which can now easily be reached inside the bottom bracket shell. After letting it work for a few minutes, proceed to extract it using a tool that I find to be essential. This tool grips the fixed cup and blocks it on the left side inside the shell. Once the wrench axle has been screwed and the cup blocked, use both hands to unscrew it. You can also do so by attaching the

ASSE

MANICOTTO

CUSCINETTI O SFERE

CALOTTA DESTRA (FISSA)

CALOTTA SINISTRA (REG.)

ANELLO DI CHIUSURA

BULLONI DI CHIUSURA

RANELLE

## BOTTOM BRACKET

- BOTTOM BRACKET
- AXLE
- SLEEVE
- BEARINGS
- FIXED CUP
- ADJUSTABLE CUP
- LOCK RING
- CLOSING NUTS
- WASHERS

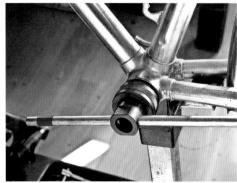

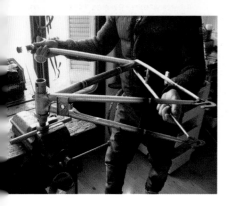

tool to the vise. By and large, removal of the fixed cup requires the most strength, and that's why you have to have the right tool to do so.

You've finally finished dismantling the individual components and can now proceed to examine each one so you can start cleaning and polishing them. Likewise, the frame is ready to be cleaned and checked, even its most delicate parts.

I've divided the bicycle in three distinct groups. The dismantled components, the frame with the fork, and the wheels. I've tried to list the most serious, troublesome problems that can be dealt with by carrying out certain procedures, but sometimes you come up against problems of a more general nature. Blunted screws, stripped threads, worn bolts... this is par for the course for anyone doing this kind of work. With experience, calm, and patience it is nonetheless possible to solve any unforeseen occurrence. Inevitably, at first you'll make some mistakes, but try not to be discouraged, and learn from your mistakes so you'll do better next time.

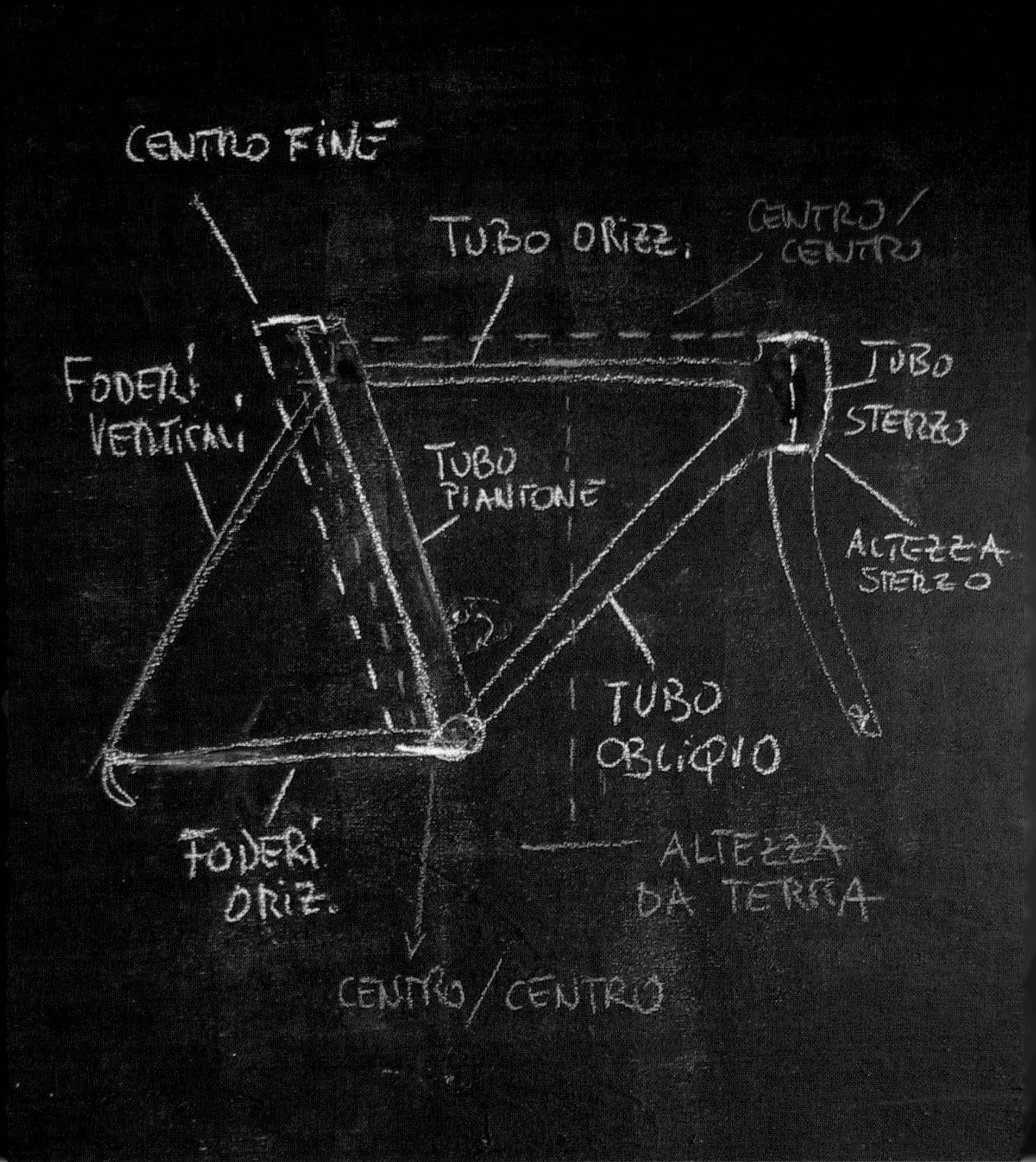

CENTRO FINE

TUBO ORIZZ.

CENTRO/CENTRO

FODERI VERTICALI

TUBO PIANTONE

TUBO STERZO

ALTEZZA STERZO

TUBO OBLIQUO

FODERI ORIZ.

ALTEZZA DA TERRA

CENTRO/CENTRO

THE VARIOUS PARTS OF THE FRAME
AND TYPES OF MEASUREMENTS
(Clockwise from the top)

– CENTER TO END
– TOP TUBE
– CENTER TO CENTER
– HEAD TUBE
– HEIGHT OF HEAD TUBE
– STANDOVER HEIGHT

– CENTER TO CENTER
– CHAIN STAYS
– SEAT STAYS
– SEAT TUBE
– DOWN TUBE

**Cleaning the frame** This is the part of the process where you have the best chance to appreciate the features of the object you have your hands on. The frame is more than the bicycle's skeleton, it is its soul, and in many cases, it is truly a work of art. You can find out whether the frame was built by a master artisan by looking at some of the details: the filings, the quality of the lugs, how accurately the tubes were assembled. In other words, once you've cleaned it, its beauty will shine through and you'll also be able to appreciate the builder's hand. In time, you'll learn to see certain details that at first go more or less unnoticed.

During this phase, you'll also be able check any damage to the frame, such as small dents, cracks, or anything else. You need to remember that the frame is constantly being submitted to stress (vibrations, oscillations, collisions...) so it's important to make sure that everything is in order. You also need to check the threads, both of the bottom bracket shell and the fork, and if it's in poor condition then go over the worn out parts. If you have the proper tool to do so, check to make sure the rear stays are aligned. In the fork, besides

the condition of the thread, make sure the tube isn't bent, crooked, or damaged in any way. See whether you can check the inside of the tubes as well to make sure there isn't any hidden rust. At this point you can start the cleaning process.

In the previous chapter we saw that there are countless cleaning products of varying quality and effectiveness. After trying out lots of them, I finally found the one that satisfied me as a degreaser for both the components and the frame. The product is made specifically for motorbikes, and it comes in the form of cotton wool soaked in a oli-based solution; it's a great degreaser without being too invasive. It's also suited to shining the parts once they've been degreased and cleaned. Besides being manageable, the product won't harm the paint and it's gentle on the decals. I suggest you try out some of the other products available to see whether you prefer to use something else, but keep in mind that even the simple combination of water and soap is both economical and effective. With a little elbow grease and lots of patience you'll be able to achieve surprising results. You should

especially be careful about the part of the frame that has the decals on it: some of them are very delicate and if you're not careful you risk ruining the colors. You also need to clean the thread inside the bottom bracket shell where lots of dirt can build up. Similarly, slide your finger into the seatpost tube, where the seatpost is inserted, and clean the inside well. If necessary go over the collar part with fine sandpaper.

If the chromed parts of the bicycle show signs of rust or oxidation, use fine glass wool or brass brushes to remove it, possibly after having rubbed the same area with a degreaser or a lubricant; by softening the build-up it will be easier to remove. If the chrome isn't cracked, then generally the rusty areas can be removed with satisfactory results.

Parts of a bicycle before and after cleaning.

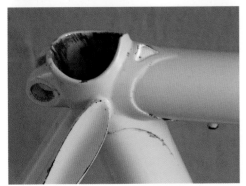

Now let's check the condition of the paint. If there is missing paint in some of the areas, you'll need to touch it up to prevent rust from forming. For this purpose, take a small brush soaked in oil or antioxidant to brush the area in question: this will create a protective film on which you can then touch up the paint. You decide whether, from an aesthetic standpoint, it's better to touch up the paint or leave the signs of age. When carrying out conservative restoration it's best to conserve the patina and simply stop the rust from getting any worse. This way you'll be preserving the original frame.

If there are no other problems to deal with, use a cloth to spread some polish on the frame. This will restore the paint's shine and prevent it from aging. Complete the job with a layer of

beeswax of the kind auto body workers use, or a silicone-based cream: besides bringing out the shine of the paint, water and sweat will slide right off without leaving any impurities. For the chromed parts as well, if there isn't any exfoliation, the chrome's original shine can also be restored. Any small signs or scratches that remain are part of the bike's history, like the wrinkles on a person's face, and they contribute to the vintage charm.

Lastly, check the micro holes on the front fork and rear stays. During construction, they were there to release any heat while welding, but if there's any dirt blocking them now they should be cleaned out to keep the air circulating inside the tubes.

Bianchi Reparto Corsa used by Ennio Vannotti
in 1983 and now owned by Wesley Hatakeyama.
Once it has been conservatively restored it will
be on display at the Eroica Cafè - Ex Cantine
Ricasoli in Gaiole in Chianti.

# A PASSION FOR CYCLING FROM CHIANTI TO THE BACK ROADS OF CALIFORNIA

*Wesley Hatakeyama*

—

A cycling enthusiast and a collector, since 2015 he is the promoter of Eroica California

My passion for road racing bicycles started when I was just eleven years old (1971) and still living partly in Japan. Watching Eddy Merckx and Felice Gimondi win the grand tours on TV as a child had a huge impact on me, and soon afterwards I joined the local junior cycling club. I continued to race as an amateur racer into the 1980s until I had to focus on my career as a professional show horse trainer. At last, in 2014, the first year of my retirement from the horse world, I was able to attend L'Eroica in Italy for the first time.

When I first arrived in Gaiole in Chianti for the 2014 L'Eroica I didn't know anyone. But I was determined to build a bike to ride in the event by finding a rare frame set (frame in my size 53cm with Campagnolo Paris Roubaix dropouts) for I had brought all the parts needed to build it from California. I was wrong about one thing though: it wasn't as easy as I thought it would be to find such a rare frame set especially in my size even at the L'Eroica bike fair. As I was searching and wandering around town, I happened to go into the Bottega L'Eroica and I asked Emanuele Nepi, the owner of the shop (and now a good friend of mine) how to find this rare frame set. He introduced me to none other than Luciano Berruti and Paolo Cavazzuti. If you're at all familiar with L'Eroica, you know we're talking about the stars of the event. As soon as they saw what I had brought from the States, they knew I was serious about finding the frame set. But there was

still one problem: it was hard for us to communicate.

While I was there, I had a chance to meet with Aki and Emi Hasegawa, the organizers of Eroica Japan (the oldest and the very first international Eroica event outside Italy) during the festival, who, in turn, introduced me to the founding members of L'Eroica. It was a key moment that set off a chain of events that took place after the ride, and the result of it was that Giancarlo Brocci traveled to Paso Robles, California to ride the proposed long heroic route and the proposed rest stops along the route. This region, San Luis Obispo County (Central Coast), is the second biggest wine-production area in California. It was early December of 2014, and only four months later, at the beginning of April 2015, the first edition of the Eroica California was held in Paso Robles, with 750 riders in attendance. The rest, as they say, is history!!

I had another passion and it was for vintage automobiles. The knowledge I gained from showing them and judging them at the major vintage Ferrari Concours d'Elegances in the U.S. led to the judging standard needed to create the proper vintage bicycle Concours, and my hope to standardize the concours judging system across the world. By bringing the serious vintage Road Racing Bicycle Concours d'Elegance to L'Eroica events, it will promote the preservation of vintage bicycles, educate the public, and establish a healthy vintage bicycle market.

**Cleaning and polishing the components** Bicycle components have evolved greatly over the years. Nowadays, they're mostly made of carbon or titanium, but until the 1990s iron/steel (especially from the early twentieth century to the mid-1950s) and aluminum (since the 1950s) were and have been mainly used. When getting ready to clean the components, you should keep this distinction in mind and be aware of the differences between the two metals. Besides weight, the most important difference lies in the way these materials age. Iron rusts, and aluminum oxidates without rusting. Generally speaking, every family of metals has its own specific cleaning product.

Soaked cotton wool, whose use I described for the frame, is specific and suited to cleaning, degreasing, and polishing a wide range of metals: brass, silver, copper, tin, aluminum, zinc, and nickel. As I said before, the product is so manageable it can easily be used for any part of the bike: it cleans metal thoroughly and carefully, it removes any oxidation without scratching, it won't build up in every nook and cranny, and, lastly, it prevents premature oxidation. In short, it's ideal for all the aluminum parts in a bike. There are various other types of degreasing products, as well as ones specifically for use on metals available on the market, without overlooking the fact that the traditional use of a brush soaked in oil is always a good (and cheap!) alternative, especially for the greasiest parts like the chain. Whichever product you choose to use, don't forget to wear protective gloves.

If, because of their condition, some of the parts need to be dismantled to be cleaned properly, don't hesitate to do so. If you're not an expert, be sure to take some pictures before taking them

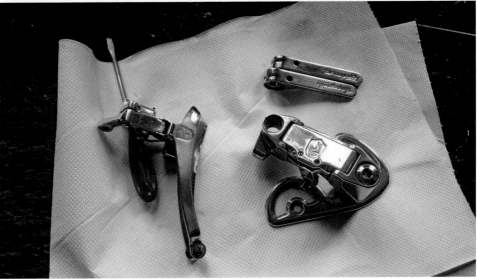

On pp. 109-11: Several components
treated with Metatrex. Here and on
p. 110 notice the difference before
and after treatment.

apart so you'll be sure to put them back together correctly. Besides your hands, to do a good job you should use all the tools you need, like brushes, sponges, steel wool, and so on. If you have a compressor you can use it to clean as well as to dry.

And even when the parts look like they're in terrible condition, don't feel discouraged: the right product, patience, and a good dose of elbow grease can work miracles.

When the glass or plastic covering the bulb of a light or headlamp has become dull, this can be fixed. Rubbing alcohol will make glass look as good as new. For plastic, instead, first rub it with fine sandpaper (1000/1500), and then polish it with paste and disk C from the kit suggested above.

Iron components get a different treatment. As iron ages it almost always gets rusty, and the rust can either stay on the surface or penetrate deep into the metal. In the former case, the rust forms orange spots that can be easily removed with oil and steel wool. In cases where the rusting is extensive, use a drill with tips for sanding combined with various types of brushes, both large and small, and sponges to reach the hardest spots. Remember that when you do this kind of work, for example sanding, and especially when you need to use a drill, gloves, goggles, and a protective mask are a must! Once you've gotten rid of all the rust, use a cloth to clean the surface and then cover it with a layer of corrosion inhibitor so that it doesn't come back.

Polishing kits to solve the toughest oxidation issues are readily
available on the market. To use these pastes and disks you'll need a
grindstone or a drill fastened to the workbench. This job isn't easy
and anyone doing it for the first time should prepare properly. You'll
also need a protective mask or goggles and gloves. The kit includes
disks and paste to be used in succession. Disks A and Z and their
relative pastes are used to remove the oxidation (pre-polishing); disk
A is used for normal oxidation, disk Z when oxidation is severe.
Disk B and its related paste is used for the polishing phase. For the
last phase (super-polishing or chrome polishing) use disk C plus
paste. Since the procedure is a messy one, it should be dealt with in
a place that you can easily clean up afterwards.

Three practical examples of the
results that can be achieved
by using a multiple disk and
matching paste kit: for the
aluminum stem and seatpost, and
the brass headlamp, the product
works on the oxidation by
eliminating it and restoring the
part to its original condition.

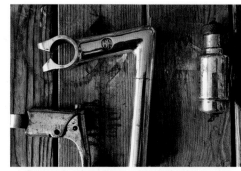

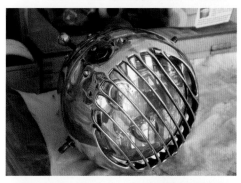

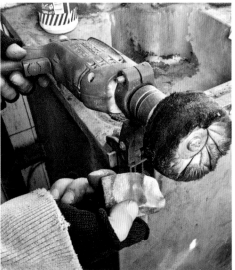

Above, an iron crank arm with its chainring where the rust has spread deep.

Below, the same components after a drill and a sandpaper disk brush were used. See the differences between before and after.

**Checking the components** After cleaning each part of the bicycle, you now have to make sure that everything works and if necessary replace what's too worn to function. Check each component individually, making sure it works and that its appearance is acceptable. This is especially true for all the parts that are more sensitive to breakage, damage, or simple wear and tear, such as the cable gear set, rubber lever hoods, toe-clip straps, handlebar tape, and saddle.

As a rule, all the bicycle's cables, for the brakes as well as for the derailleurs, should be replaced with new ones. For all the other parts, a decision will have be made each time a problem comes up. Start from the housing, whose importance we mustn't underestimate because it influences whether the cables work properly and, as a result, whether the brakes or the derailleurs do, too. Check the rubber housing: if there are any tears that let you see the steel spring underneath, then the housing will have to be replaced. As for the brake levers, check the state of the

rubber hoods, and, again, if there are any cuts or tears they'll need to be replaced. Note, however, that not all the hood models are still available on the market. As for the brake calipers, the first thing you need to check is the condition of the springs: tug on the caliper to see if the spring has the right pull. If the caliper arms don't move properly, lubricate the axle located close to the closing bolt. Check whether the brake pads are worn and if so replace them. As for the handlebar and stem, make sure there aren't any cracks and that the handlebar is inclined the way it was originally. If the tape is in poor condition or too worn, replace it. Check the rear derailleur to make sure the two jockey wheels are in working order; most of the time they're made of plastic so it's likely they'll be cracked or worn. If the pedals have toe-clips and straps, make sure they're in satisfactory condition. In the past, the straps were easily broken, so it's common to see damage at the base of the toe-clips. The saddle is another part of the bike that's prone to wear and aging.

Make sure nothing is broken under the shell and that the material used for the cover is in good condition. Judging the appearance of the saddle is very subjective. Personally, I don't mind seeing minor abrasions and the normal signs of wear that are visible on aged leather. Actually, I think they have a certain vintage charm.

If some of these parts have to be replaced, remember to choose the right one because that's the first rule of conservative restoration. This is also true for the parts that are often overlooked, such as the housing and the handlebar tape. I've often noticed "mistakes" in this type of conservative restoration. These things might seem unimportant, but ultimately they make all the difference between a professional restoration and a more amateurish one. For instance, it's embarrassing from an aesthetic point of view to see a 1970s bike with a carbon saddle or a cork handlebar tape. Not to mention the fact that handlebar tape, cable housing, straps, and toe-clips are all inexpensive.

After analyzing these sensitive parts, you need to check the ones that play a mechanical role, that is to say, the ball bearings. They're located in the headset, the bottom bracket, the pedals, the hubs, and the freewheel. In this case as well, when there is excessive wear, replace them without giving it a second thought.

In the headset check the ball bearings and the cages that contain them, making sure they're in good condition and that there's no rust. As for the races, check the surfaces where the ball bearings slide in, both the ones attached to the frame and the ones that have been dismantled: the surfaces should show no signs of pitting or grinding marks. Checking the bottom bracket is similar to checking the headset, i.e. check the condition of the bearing surfaces inside the races to make sure that they show no signs of pitting or grinding marks. The same needs to be done for the part corresponding to the axle, i.e. where the bearings turn. Here again there should be no grinding marks or wear. Should you notice that

the axle or the races aren't perfect then it's best to replace them. It's easy to check the condition of the pedals: all you have to do is hold them in your hand and make sure they spin on the axle. If that is not the case, then remove the caps and check the state of the grease and the bearings. As for the hubs, make sure they slide easily: use two fingers to grasp the two spindle washers while making the wheel turn. If it doesn't turn easily or tends to slow down, then you'll have to take them apart to examine the condition of the hubs more closely. We'll take a closer look at this in Chapter Six. To evaluate the rotation of the freewheel use your fingers to turn the freewheel counter-clockwise. If it doesn't turn properly, then it's best to lubricate the inside of the intersection between the body and the splines. This procedure will also be examined more in detail in Chapter Six when we discuss the wheels.

Lastly, if you need to replace the headset or the bottom bracket, make sure you take detailed notes on each component. For the headset you'll need to check the type of thread (French, Italian, etc.) and the height. For the bottom bracket you'll need to measure the outside and inside length of the axle and the type of thread for the races. In this case as well, if you're to follow the rules of conservative restoration, make sure you find the matching part in terms of brand and type.

**Greasing and assembling the components**
Once you've cleaned the frame and checked all the components, you're ready to assemble your bike. This is unquestionably the part I like the best about the whole restoration process. It's the moment when you finally see the results of all your efforts, when the precision work begins that will put all the individual components back together as if they were the gears of a clock. Just as you did for the dismantling phase, you're going to need certain specific tools. The path you need to follow to assemble the components is essentially the

reverse of the one you followed to take them apart. A detailed discussion about the tools and products required can be found in Chapter Three, so I'm just going to add a short note here about the lubricant to use to grease some of the components: use a high-quality product that will do a good job. I'm talking from experience. High lubrication, anti-corrosion, and anti-wear properties will guarantee the greatest amount of resistance to mechanical loading and they are highly recommended for ball bearings and all moving parts.

After making sure you have all the components you need, especially the ones that will replace some of the parts—of essential importance if you don't want to have to stop midway through the job! —it's time to get started.

Start by mounting the headset and fasten the fork to the frame. Grease the races, both the one still attached to the frame and the one that's been taken apart. Then grease the bearings and reposition them inside the races. After that insert the fork inside the head tube and, after greasing the thread, screw in the adjustable race, adjust the washer (careful to fit it into the fork tube properly), and, lastly, tighten the lock nut. To make sure you've tightened the headset enough manually check that all the mechanisms turn freely, that is, without catching or showing excessive looseness. The fork should turn properly without any knocking or play.

Now move on to the assembly of the bottom bracket and the first thing you need to do is use your finger or a brush to spread some grease or lubricant on the thread inside the bottom bracket shell. Then fill the fixed cup with grease, insert the bearings, and cover them with grease as far as the rim of the cup; then use your hands to screw them so that they go perfectly with the thread. If the race doesn't enter the shell perfectly, don't force it, otherwise you'll risk ruining the thread. If you're having problems the best thing to do is unscrew it and try to understand why you can't screw it in; continue trying until the thread fits perfectly. Once the fixed cup has been screwed in perfectly and is correctly joined to the shell, use the proper wrench to lock it. Now, once you've locked the fixed cup, move over to the left side and insert the protective sleeve and the axle in the hole of the fixed cup. Make sure the axle is in the right direction (the long part goes inside the fixed cup). Grease the adjustable race, which is inserted by hand, screwing it in carefully. To wind up with a perfect (or nearly perfect) adjustment, after you've closed the fixed cup and are about to tighten the adjustable race, rotate the

axle, which should rotate free of any bearing friction, with a small amount of tolerance accepted.

In this procedure a little play is preferable to excessive closing. Complete the adjustment by screwing the lock ring up to the bottom bracket shell, at the same time using the special bottom bracket wrenches to make sure that everything has been properly adjusted.

After adjusting and closing the bottom bracket, you're ready to put the crank arms back in place. Insert the right crank arm followed by the left crank arm in the square taped axle, then screw the bolts, followed by the caps.

After you've reassembled the crank arm move on to the pedals. If they don't rotate properly check the state of the cage bearings using a special wrench to open them. After removing the

cap check the state of the grease. The best thing to do is clean all the bearings and grease them over again, making sure that the rotation is perfect and smooth before closing them up again. For the sake of convenience, any toe-clips and straps should be assembled to the pedals before they're screwed onto the crank arm.

Now let's move on to the break calipers, both front and rear, greasing the closing axle for each one. If the bike has fenders remember to assemble them at the same time as the calipers.

After the brakes, if present, assemble the derailleur set, attaching the shifting levers to the frame, then the front and rear derailleurs. Use oil to lubricate the pivot point of the front derailleur and the jockey wheels of the rear derailleur. A word on the front derailleur and the shifting

levers: if you're working on a "clamp on" model, try to reposition them on the marks left previously.

Now let's move on to the handlebar, the stem, and the brake levers. Out of habit, and for the sake of convenience, I personally assemble these three components on the workbench before inserting them in the frame. Remember to clean the stem and grease the expander or wedge. Once you've done that, insert the stem and the levers inside the fork steerer tube and clamp the bolt. Then use a yardstick to make sure the brake levers are attached in the correct position.

All that's left to do now is assemble the seatpost and saddle. Generously grease the seatpost tube and use a finger to grease the inside collar of the seat tube. Then insert the seatpost and center the saddle in line with the handlebar stem. Use a bubble level tool to correct the degree of inclination, and adjust the seatpost so that it's the right height. Lastly, close the binder bolt and use some paper to remove any excess grease around the collar.

The moment has come to assemble all the new cables and housing for the brakes and derailleurs. Let's start from the housing. If it's been changed, take the necessary measurements before cutting them so they're the right length,

then clip them to the frame top tube with gear clips or insert them in the cable guides brazed on the frame. The same goes for the derailleur housing. In this case remember to grease the cable guides brazed on the frame or under the bottom bracket shell so that they move smoothly and to prevent any fraying from occuring.

Let's finish the job by assembling the chain and then the wheels, and then adjusting the brake pads and the derailleurs. If you've decided to replace the handlebar tape, then that's the last step. Wear white gloves to avoid leaving dirty fingerprints. The handlebar, saddle, and wheels are examined more in depth in Chapter Six.

Now you can step away from the bicycle and observe your work with satisfaction. Analyze each component as well as the results as a whole. If you're not happy with some of your aesthetic choices, re-examine them with a critical eye. Sometimes when you look at the bicycle as a whole, you end up changing your mind about the type of saddle or handlebar tape you chose. Don't hesitate to replace or change things that aren't completely satisfactory. Don't rush to finish a job if there's something that doesn't convince you. This is often the right time to judge your work and, if necessary, make improvements.

**Finishing touches, photographic record, test**
The reassembled bicycle is ready for the finishing touches, to be photographed, and to be tested. When everything has been assembled use paper to clean any dirt or fingerprints on the frame, and add one last layer of polish to protect and enhance the paint. If the saddle is made of leather, then add another layer of leather grease to make it shine. Wipe all the components with cotton cloth so that they sparkle like jewelry. If you haven't replaced the tubulars or the tires and the originals are still on the bike, use one of the many products available to make the rubber look brand

new. Use the same product on all the rubber parts, for example, the brake pads and the hoods.

Once you've added the finishing touches, you can mount the bike on a stand against a solid background and take pictures of it. Pictures are important for several reasons. They create an archive of your work, and they can also be used as a reference for later restorations. Pictures can help us improve, and if we share them they can be used by other bike and restoration enthusiasts.

But not just that: we can finally compare them with the pictures taken at the beginning and admire the differences before and after the

On pp. 126-29: A 1940s French Aviac. The pictures and the work that was done on it highlight the beauty of the finishings as well as of the bike itself.

restoration. As a matter of fact, before photographing the restored bike I suggest looking at the initial pictures so that the new ones resemble them as closely as possible. Just as you did at the beginning, focus on the details and the bike overall so as to have a general view of the work done.

Lastly, the moment has come to road test our work: it's important to take a test ride on your restored bike to make sure that everything is the way it should be. Make sure the brakes, the bottom bracket, and the headset are in perfect working order, and check to see that the gears are properly adjusted.

Here and on the following
page, the final pictures after the
conservative restoration of a
French Rochet from the 1950s.
The beauty of the overall shapes
and details is clearly visible.

Here and on the previous page, two examples of final pictures that let you to admire the work done with satisfaction: a Colnago Master Equilatero chronometer and a CBT Italia from the 1970s.

# TOTAL AND CREATIVE RESTORATION

Example of the total restoration of a Gloria La Garibaldina.
The bicycle was made to look as close to the original as possible.
Though the Gloria featured nickel plating of the frame, this was
not carried out here. A coat of transparent varnish achieved an
effect that came close to the original.

T hough I generally prefer conservative restoration, in certain situations I'm forced to carry out total restoration. You might find yourself, for example, with a frame that had previously been painted in a slipshod manner, or in such poor condition that conservative restoration wouldn't be enough to give it an acceptable aesthetic appearance. In cases such as these, total restoration is the best choice, involving repainting of the frame.

Before starting, we need to discuss decals. If the plan is to carry out a total restoration of the bike, then you'll need to make sure that decals matching its model and type are available somewhere. Repainting a frame and leaving it "bare," without decals, isn't a good solution from an aesthetic point of view, because you end up with a bicycle that's anonymous as a whole.

However, the above doesn't apply in creative restoration. You're free to choose because the final goal isn't restoring the bike to its original state but simply giving it a brand new look. Most creative restorations don't require original decals, and are actually more effective if they clearly reveal "our own" personalization. In restorations such as these, decals are applied freely. You run into lots of these more or less everywhere, especially in the fixed gear world where personalization has become the norm.

**Removing the paint from the frame** All the dismantling and cleaning phases that I described for conservative restoration also apply in total restoration. In addition, the latter also involves repainting the frame, as well as re-doing the chrome plating on any components that you think needs it. In creative restoration as well, painting or treatment of the frame is almost a must; you'll also be free to choose, change, and replace all the components, thus recreating the bicycle of your dreams.

But let's take a step back and return for a moment to the dismantling phase, and more specifically to the headset. In the chapter on conservative restoration, we discussed dismantling one part of the headset, avoiding the complete removal of the races still attached to the frame and the one connected to the fork. While this operation could be omitted in conservative restoration, for total restoration you're going to have to completely dismantle these three pieces as well.

Once you've removed the frame and the fork from the headset, you can start stripping the paint and getting the frame ready for a new paint job. There are various ways to remove the paint, the most common being paint stripping and dry sanding. If you're on a limited budget paint stripping is the best choice because you can do it yourself. Otherwise sanding is a good choice, and it can be done by a professional after they've given you a cost estimate. Usually, the cost of sanding a frame and a fork won't be high because a professional will be able to do the job in a couple of minutes. However, if you decide to remove the paint yourself it's going to require much more in terms of time and effort. I'd say that hiring a professional for some of the phases of a total restoration is essential if you want to achieve good quality. I especially advise against the DIY approach when it comes to sanding and painting.

If you decide to strip the paint yourself, there are two techniques to choose from: either dry, or with the help of a chemical product. In any case, before starting be sure to take the necessary precautions, which means wearing rubber gloves, a protective mask, goggles, and suitable clothing. For dry removal of the paint the frame has to be stabilized properly. You'll also need a drill, a set of

## DISASSEMBLY OF THE RACES ATTACHED TO THE FRAME AND FORK

The photographs on the blackboard show the tools used to extract the crown race of the headset attached to the fork. The tool you'll want to use to do this is the U-shaped one visible in photo 1. After placing it inside the head of the fork with its extremities against the race, one blow with a hammer should make the race slide out of the tube (photo 2). The specific tool for extracting the top and bottom races attached to the headtube of the frame is instead the tube with a fan-like extremity visible in photo 3. Inserted inside the headtube, the fan gets caught on the inner thickness of the race, and once again a blow of the hammer will be enough to make it come out (photo 4). Repeat for the other race.

brushes, tips, and various types of abrasive discs to reach all the nooks and crannies.

Chemical removal of the paint instead requires purchasing any one of the good paint stripping products readily available on the market. Until 2011 these products contained methylene chloride, later banned because it's toxic. Strip paint removers available on the market today are "DMC-free." They come in gel form and are aromatic as well as biodegradable, but should still be used outdoors. Take a brush and spread the gel over the entire surface of the frame and fork (front and back, top and bottom). Let the gel do its job, then use metal brushes and spatulas to remove the larger areas of peeled paint. Smaller spatulas and brushes can be used to remove the paint residue that's harder to get at. Lastly, wipe the areas where the paint has been stripped with a cloth soaked in alcohol or paint thinner.

At this point all the construction details will be apparent on the frame—serial number, measurements, manufacturer's signature, welding, filing, etc.—that were previously hidden from sight. If you're working on several frames at the same time, before repainting you might want to compare these "bare" details by taking pictures of them and saving them for later reference and/or for your files. For instance, often the serial number etched on the frame can also be found on the fork steerer tube, proof that the two pieces are original.

The stripping process is always the same whether you're working on an aluminum or a steel frame, but based on my experience I suggest using a dry method when you're dealing with aluminum, along with brushes and abrasive disks attached to a drill. Aluminum is softer, more delicate, and the use of chemical agents is unnecessary. Good abrasive brushes will achieve results that are more than satisfactory, even for the parts that are the hardest to reach.

Sanding, which is the other technique used to remove paint, is a mechanical process in which the uppermost layer of a material is eroded by blasting it

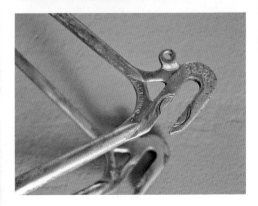

On pp. 142-45: This 1950s Bianchi underwent total restoration.
The complete bicycle before and after restoration, the same
situation in several details. Even the water bottles were painted
the same color as the frame.

Right: Chicco, my trusty
sander as he gets ready
to finish a job.

Previous page: Two details
before and after painting.

After sanding and stripping, several details are visible on the frame that couldn't be seen before. This is also when spot putty is added (below left).

with sand and air. There are various types, the most common of which, for metals, is dry with white metal sanding. The result of this is a frame with a uniform gray-white metal surface and roughness that depends on the size of the grit used.

Personally, if I'm working on a single frame I choose paint stripping. However, if I've decided to hire a professional, then I try to make the most of the time and cost required by waiting until I have several frames so they can be dealt with all at once.

As concerns creative restoration, sometimes paint stripping or sanding aren't necessary. It all depends on the results you want to achieve. I've seen many cases, especially with fixed-gear city bikes, where a DIY paint job with spray cans was carried out, and the outcome was aesthetically acceptable overall. When you aim to "recreate" a bicycle that reflects your taste, you can try out solutions that are an alternative to a simple and uniform paint job. This is the case, for instance, when you're looking for rough effects like "rust," "asphalt," or even a *trompe l'œil* faux wood effect.

Sanding is also useful when you're forced to chrome some of the parts of the frame. In this case, too, be sure to outsource the work to companies specialized in galvanization, provided that, before being submitted to a galvanic process, the individual components and the frame have been professionally sanded or paint-stripped. Also bear in mind that galvanization is not cheap, so make sure you're properly informed before going ahead with it.

Lastly, when you've completely stripped the paint or sanded down the frame, besides admiring the bare details, you'll be able to see whether there are any dents or flaws in the metal of the tubes.

If that's the case, then this is the right time to touch up and fix the frame, before moving on to the painting stages. Special stucco kits for metal are available on the market, generally used for motorbikes or musical instruments. Stucco is a doughy paste to which a small amount of hardener must be added. Use a metal or plastic spatula to spread it on the frame and, after it has hardened, ordinary sandpaper can be used to smooth it and even it out.

**Choice of color and decals** Having reached this stage, before moving on to the actual paint job, you'll need to decide which color and which decals you'd like to use. For creative restoration, the choice is a personal one and there is no rule to follow other than that of personal taste. A lot of the fun in reconstructing a bicycle according to you own whims and fancies lies in this freedom of action. Instead, total restoration requires us to follow, wherever possible, the original color palette and to use decals matching the bicycle's model and type. This is a detail that should not be underestimated: it is not unusual to see total restorations with the wrong decals. If you have no reference for the frame before stripping the paint off, you can search the Internet or old catalogs to get the information you need on the right type of stickers. The same brand of bicycle can show variations depending on the year of production, and it's important to be aware of these differences. On the market you can find specific decals of many types, but be careful, because while there are many who claim to be specialized sellers, not all of them offer excellent quality and a wide range of brands. One of the most renowned, serious, and well-stocked professionals in this field is Greg Softley, who runs a very popular online store at the address www.cyclomondo.net. With a bit of luck, you can also find original decals or original reproductions at bicycle trade fairs and shows. Also keep in mind that a good graphic artist will be able to reproduce any decal for you based on photographic references. However, the process is a costly one and not always worthwhile. If you're lucky enough to find original decals that are right for the model you're restoring, check the condition they're in. In time, the paper or glue may have been altered by humidity, and the sun and light may have damaged the intensity of the colors.

For the most important, famous brands, there are multiple color combinations for the same set of decals. This should be kept in mind

because it will affect the choice of paint color. If you chose a light color for the paint job, then the decals should be of a dark shade, and vice versa. Furthermore, the existence of a wide range of decal colors expands the possible combinations you can create with the paint job and the details, such as the color of the cable gears or the handlebar tape. For the choice of color it's customary in total restorations to comply with the color palette that the brand had in its catalog, and the same reference will be useful for the combination of decals. If the frame you've paint-stripped had its original color, then you can use that as reference, although you're not forced to. With total restoration you also have the chance to vary the color, as long as it's one of the colors available when the bike was being produced.

When you're looking for color references for less-well-known or older bikes, it's often hard to get the information you need. The best thing to do in cases such as these is to find out what colors were being used for cars. If you know the year the bike was manufactured, you can find which colors were popular for cars back then. In the 1940s and '50s there were very few colors available, but in the 1980s the range of colors was practically endless. For the most important brands (for instance, Bianchi) you can find the exact paint codes used at specific times. However, if you plan to repaint your frame with a particular effect, using *cromovelatura* or two-component painting, then you should ask the painter beforehand whether he thinks the results will be satisfactory and how much it's going to cost.

Lastly, here are two more things to remember. First, besides decals, a frame might also have metal head badges. This is especially true of pre-1960s bikes. Many of them can still be found in the markets, and luckily the ones for the most important brands are still being produced. Second, if some of the frame components need to be chrome plated, be sure to do that before painting the frame.

# THE GRAND RESTORATION REVIVAL

*Greg Softley*

—

A collector and restorer for two decades, he is the promoter of Cyclomondo,
supplier of high-quality decals and classic bicycle components

How does one convince those that are not obsessed already, to see the beauty, art, craftsmanship and mechanical genius of these significant hand-built bicycles? I believe that the wonderful pictures in the pages of this book can do so more than a thousand words. Neglected, used and abused bicycles are aplenty and these feed the appetite of the growing numbers of classic bicycle restorers. The restorer's craft is now repopulating the streets, and there are classic riding events, and personal collections with bicycles of superior build quality compared with the original products of the day. The sheer joy of undertaking a historically correct and sometimes significant restoration is totally addictive. Easy restorations lead to personal challenges where eventually the most difficult and rare examples are sought. The near unobtainable components for these projects can sometimes take years to source and the gathering of correct resource material is an adventure in it-

self. The finished product is a statement of triumph. A work of art. A window to history and old technology. A pure example of form and function. These bicycles are also a testament to the heroic achievements of the competitive riders of the past. Restorers have no geographical boundaries. They live on every continent and in every country on the planet. The Internet has provided a platform where the sharing of ideas, sources for parts, reference for build specifications and technical processes are at our fingertips. The web has also created a global network where classic bicycle aficionados can enjoy and share in a worldwide social network unavailable to previous generations. When looking at the masterpieces of mechanics and engineering shown on these pages, it's hard to resist the temptation to unleash your creative talents and, after bringing an old heirloom back to life, hop back on the saddle and pedal away!

**Toward finalizing the job** Once the frame has been sanded down, the decals have been bought, the color chosen, you're ready to move on to the last stage of the project.

As already mentioned, it's a good idea to have the paint job done by a professional, if possible someone who's an expert when it comes to bicycle frames. A normal auto body worker is accustomed to painting flat surfaces, while a bicycle frame requires attention to details and skilled hands. That same professional, based on his or her experience, will often suggest colors and solutions for your projects. In some rare cases, I have even been lucky enough to run into the same artisans who once did paint jobs for famous brands. They turned out to be excellent consultants for the choice of color and the decals, too, and besides having the original codes, often they can show you samples with the different combinations of decals and colors directly on the tubes.

On the contrary, you won't necessarily have to outsource a paint job to a professional when you're working on a creative restoration project. The beauty of this type of restoration is precisely the fact that you can do everything with your own hands, giving free rein to your imagination using the frame as a base. The purpose of creative restoration is not to restore the original state of the bicycle, but to transform it by creating something new, something unique. The only thing you want to make sure you do, should you want to try out certain paints or special effects like cracking, rust, or other chemical processes, is test a piece of iron first rather than going directly to the frame.

A professional paint job includes all the phases, from the laying of the undercoat to the

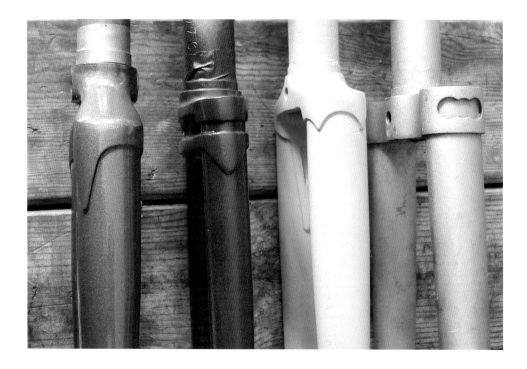

final varnishing, and it is undoubtedly the costliest part of the restoration. I suggest requesting a cost estimate to avoid any unpleasant surprises, especially when, in addition to painting, you're looking at chrome plating, masks, lining, shades, and other details. Any requests that go beyond the standard will make the cost of the restoration go up.

The time for the decals has finally come. Once, they used to be applied after the final varnishing, but that left them fragile and unprotected; nowadays bike restorers prefer to apply them before the two coats of transparent varnish to avoid the risk of their coming off or fading. This is also true for creative restoration, where funny stickers and decals, sometimes outlandish ones, are popular. If you finish off the job by applying a colorless fixative the product of your creativity will last longer.

Before discussing the paint cycles and the application of the decals more in detail, one more thing needs to be said about the person doing the painting. Try to locate a professional who works in your area, not just for the sake of convenience, but also to avoid wasting money in shipping costs. But besides that, it will also give you a chance to see with your own eyes how they work, and if you need a touch-up in the future, they'll be easy to reach.

A series of frames on which an epoxy undercoat was applied before painting, and, more specifically, close-ups showing the type of primer finishing before the paint is sprayed on.

**The painting stages** Now, let's examine all the painting stages in a sequence starting from the anchoring undercoat. The epoxy base is a primer formulated with anti-corrosive and antirust resins, which has a considerable amount of anchoring power on different materials, such as iron, aluminum, cast iron, etc. It is sprayed directly onto the frame after it has been sanded, and it creates the base for the subsequent paint job. It's available on the market in a number of shades, light gray, brick red, and white being the ones most used. The difference in the shade of the undercoat depends on the choice of the definitive color: if you've chosen a light color, then the undercoat should be white; for all the in-between shades a light gray undercoat is recommended;

lastly, brick red is suited to dark shades. If the frame has some chrome plating, metal head badges or other details that shouldn't be painted, these should be covered before applying the epoxy base.

Once the opaque color has been sprayed on, it's time for the finishing, the decals, the masks for the logos, or for you to create grid effects or shades. Before applying any masks, use steel wool or sandpaper to make the frame surface rough enough for the masks to stick to the surface more easily. This is especially important when metallic paint was used. The mask has a hard time adhering to metallic paint. After spray painting the base color it's time to do some paint finishing, such as going over the

Here and on the previous page,
some of the steps for using
masking tape while painting.

pantography or engravings and, if appropriate, proceeding with the lining as well. As for the latter, not all painters are capable of doing a good job. I have personally met several specialists, abolute expert painters of lining, but there aren't many of them. Back in the day, especially in the 1940s and '50s, there were people—often women—who only did this type of work, using special brushes to paint the lining on the frame. It was a job that required a certain skill and technique, besides a steady hand. A meticulous and repetitive job that gave the frame that "hand-painted" feel and uniqueness that no longer exists. Nowadays, it's not easy to find people capable of doing this kind of finishing, although in the wake of the vintage bicycle revival and the rise in the number of enthusiasts the situation seems to be improving.

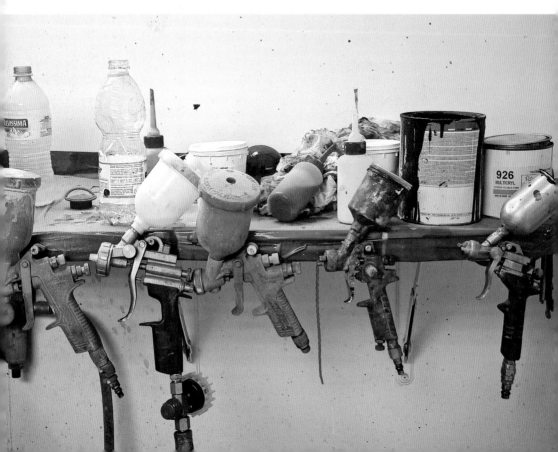

Here and on the following page: Example of creative restoration: "Eggshell white" women's bike. The basket, fenders, and chainguard were painted the same color as the frame. The inside of the chainguard was painted black to make the chrome crank arm stand out. The skirt savers are black and white, matching the rest of the bike.

Some examples of De Rosa
brand dry transfers.

**Types of decals** There are substantially three types of decal reproductions on the bicycle market: classic stickers, wet decals, and dry transfers. To apply each of these types specific actions are required. You'll also need a cutter, a pair of scissors, a tape measure, some masking tape, and several sheets of fine sandpaper (1000/1500).

To apply wet decals you'll need to buy some colorless additive-free copal paint (e.g. Damar) and a brush to apply it. Generally speaking, these come in the form of paper backing with a layer of film to which the decal is attached. Before applying the decal, you need to prepare the area on the frame, using fine sandpaper to make it slightly rough. After that, cut off the excess paper

around the decal and peel it off the backing. Now you have the film with the decal attached to it. Use a fine-tipped brush to apply Damar paint to it. Wait a few seconds for the paint to turn gluey and then apply the decal to the frame, rubbing it and pressing it carefully so that it sticks to the entire surface. If need be, use elastic bands to keep it in place. When the film is perfectly attached to the frame, leave it there for at least eight hours so the paint will dry and keep the decal glued to the bike. Once the drying time has ended, remove the film from the decal which should in the meantime have become attached to the frame. To remove the film, take a cloth or sponge and a basin of luke-warm water. Soak and pat the film just slightly,

repeating several times until the film comes off the frame. Don't try to remove the film before it's ready because you might end up ruining the decal underneath. Once the film has been removed, leave the decal to dry without touching it for a couple of days, after which you can finish the job with a couple of coats of colorless varnish.

Decals commonly known as "dry transfers" are essentially a sheet that's thermal-printed in a dry printing process that makes the colors bright and protects them from UV rays. With this kind of decal, the use of colorless varnish is advisable but not essential. If you find it hard to detach the decal from the backing, try using a cutter or pin to raise it up from the border, if necessary moistening it ever so slightly. To position it correctly, use a tape measure and masking tape.

The first rule for applying dry transfers is this: don't soak them in water. The second rule is: don't soak them in water! Decals of this sort have waterproof adhesive and are fundamentally of the peel off and stick type. That being said, there are some important passages that need to be complied with to make this procedure simple and effective. Use a pair of scissors to cut out the individual decals on the same sheet, careful not to touch the printed area. Continue by preparing the area on the frame, using fine sandpaper to make it slightly rough. Once the sanded down part has been cleaned, you're ready to apply the decals. This can be done in one of two ways: using a "wet" method or a "dry" one.

For the dry application of the decal use a dry frame. The advantage of using this method is that once you've applied the decals the frame is practically ready to be varnished; the disadvantage is that there is no margin of error—once it's fixed, the decal can't be moved. The "wet" method is instead an easier technique, because it lets you make some small adjustments while you're doing the job. However, if you have to varnish the frame as well, you'll have to wait at least a week for all the moisture to disappear.

To apply a decal on a wet frame, moisten the surface of the frame where the decal is to be attached. Peel the decal from the backing and apply it to the damp part of the frame. Because the area is wet, the decal will slide on the frame and you'll be able to put it in the right place and eliminate any air bubbles. Leave it to dry for several hours, then remove the transparent film.

For dry application, make the part of the frame where the decal will go slightly rough, as indicated above. Peel off the backing and carefully apply the decal to the frame. Use a tape measure and masking tape if necessary, so as to have accurate references on the frame. After applying the decal rub it thoroughly and let it rest for a couple of hours. Lastly, when you're sure it's properly attached to the frame, remove the transparent film.

For decals that resemble classic stickers, make sure no air bubbles form when you remove the backing. This is best done by exerting slight outwards pressure during the whole application phase, and removing the backing as the decal is unrolled onto the frame.

**The varnishing** Once you've finished adding all the decals to the frame, you can move on to the last painting stage: the application of clear-coat varnish. You'll need at least a couple of coats, sometimes three, to get a "glassy" effect and accentuate the depth of the color. Be sure to sand the frame with moistened 1500 sandpaper in between coats. Over time, I've started to get the hang of the color intensity, especially when it concerns a metallic color: after the clear coat is applied, some colors stand out more than others. This has nothing to do with the results of the job, it actually depends on their basic make-up.

When the day finally comes for me to go pick up the frame I'm always very excited about seeing the final results. That's the moment of truth, and only then will you know whether or not you've done a good job.

The final color of the bike after the clear-coat varnish has been applied isn't always the same. Some colors stand out more than others. See how the color green in this picture is shinier and has a greater metallic effect compared to the color red.

On pp. 168-69: After repainting the frame, leftover paint and decals can also be used to complete some of the accessories: water bottles, fenders, chainguards, pumps… these are typical accessory kits that can be included in the paint job in order to make the restoration seem more complete.

On pp. 170-73: The total restoration of a 1980s De Rosa.

On pp. 174-77: This ivory men's Colnago underwent total restoration. The pantographs on the frame were painted yellow, like the cable gear, with the same color tonality as the frame.

On pp. 178-81:
The creative restoration
of two women's bikes.

# WHEELS, SADDLE, AND HANDLEBAR

6

If you look at a bicycle as a whole you will notice that the wheels, the saddle, and the handlebar are perhaps the three components that most influence the overall aesthetic impact. So when you're carrying out the conservative restoration of a bike these three components are very important. This is why I've decided to devote a chapter only to them.

**The wheels** The wheels are among the most often modified and replaced components in a bicycle, so the first thing you need to do is check the congruency of their individual parts. A wheel consists of four different pieces joined together: rubber (tubular or tire), the rim, the hub, and the spokes, with corresponding washers and nipples. In addition to this, the rear wheel has a single gear or a freewheel with cogs. All these elements need to be analyzed in terms of how they work together, as well as individually.

The first thing to do is check that the wheels really are a "pair," or whether something has changed. Check to see whether the four components listed above are of the same brand and model for both the front and rear wheel. Most importantly, check the skewers for the hubs, the so-called quick release, and the tires or tubulars, the two components that are most often replaced. If one of the components isn't original, you'll have to replace it, even if this means rebuilding the entire wheel.

After you've made sure the parts go together, check the technical and aesthetic features by examining each wheel individually. First, grip the hub washers between your fingers and make the wheel spin, checking that it moves properly, that is, straight and smooth. This tells you that the hub bearings are in good shape. If there's a freewheel on the rear wheel, use your fingers to make it spin so you can check whether it's still working smoothly. It's usually very dirty so you'll have to disassemble it to be able to clean it and grease it properly.

To remove the rear wheel's freewheel you'll need a particular extractor (known as a puller) depending on the model. As there are various types, if you don't have the proper wrench this can be a problem. Instead, you should have no difficulty reassembling the freewheel once you've finished cleaning it: all you need to do is screw the freewheel onto the hub, even without a wrench, because the centrifugal force produced when the bicycle moves will make sure the whole thing is fastened tight.

Dismantling the freewheel gives you the chance to clean the rear hub and the spokes thoroughly, otherwise they're hard to get at. The products used to clean the hubs, spokes, and rims are the same as the ones described in the previous chapters for all the components. Any cyclist who has just polished his bike and then gone for a ride on a well-lit street will tell you how beautiful and gratifying it is to see the sparkle of wheels that look brand new, kissed by the sun.

As for the spokes, let's first of all check the shape they're in and make sure there's no rust. If there's only a small amount of rust it can easily be removed with glass wool or steel wool. If, instead, the rust goes deep, I advise replacing the spokes entirely. Only when it's impossible to find the right spokes with their corresponding nipples—this is usually the case when the bicycle was made in the 1930s or even before—will you be forced to try to restore the spokes even when they're very rusty. Whether or not to replace the spokes with new ones is a personal decision, based on your own aesthetic evaluations and your own appraisal of the overall condition of the wheels. Obviously, when you're restoring a bike conservatively you should try to save as much of the original material as you can; however, this isn't always possible or satisfying from an aesthetic standpoint. Allow me to say that if you do decide to replace the spokes, mechanically speaking the assembly and truing of a wheel is undoubtedly one of the most difficult, delicate steps in a restoration, so if you're not an expert, it's best to get a professional to help you out.

If while checking the hubs you noticed some friction and the wheel doesn't turn smoothly, then you'll have to clean the hub bearings. To open the hubs and reach the ball bearings use the right kind of flat wrench to unscrew the washers blocking the axle. After opening the hub and removing the axle, check the condition of the surfaces and the bearings. Just as we said previously for the headset

This series of pictures shows how to extract the freewheel. After removing the quick release, insert the puller into the body (photo 1) so that the "bosses" (prongs) match up to the notches. To make sure that it doesn't come out while you're trying to remove the freewheel, use the quick release nut (photo 2) to block it. At this point you can use a normal wrench to unscrew it, or you can lock the extractor in a vise and make the wheel spin (photo 3), careful to open the quick release at the same time. Once you've unscrewed the freewheel (photo 4), you'll have no trouble cleaning it. Should it be seized you can use lubricant to unblock it, allowing it to filter inside the mechanism of the body.

After opening the hubs, clean
them all over, not just the
surfaces (photo 1); clean the
axle too (photo 2). Don't forget
to check the skewers, and if
their levers are a bit jammed,
grease the mechanisms,
allowing the lubricant to
penetrate well (photo 3). Do
the same for the body after the
freewheel has been reassembled
(photo 4).

Sometimes when you're not an expert it's hard to understand what all the numbers printed on a bicycle tire refer to. The white part of the one in the picture reads: "35 x 590 650 x 35A 26 x 1 3/8." This is the tire's size, expressed according to the three most common systems. The first series (35 x 590) is the one corresponding to the ETRTO system: 35 refers to the width in millimeters, and 590 to the diameter in millimeters inside the rim. The second piece of information (650 x 35A) is based on the French system: 650 refers to the outer diameter of the rim (approximately), and 35 to the width of the tire in millimeters. The third piece of information (26 x 1 3/8) is based on the English system and it is in inches: the outer diameter of the rim measures 26 inches (approximately), and the width of the tire is 1 3/8 inches.

and the bottom bracket, replace both the bearings and the axle if they're worn, or even the entire hub. After generously greasing all these components, reassemble the hub, careful to leave a certain degree of tolerance that, if not respected, could affect the fluidity. Note that for this maintenance procedure you don't need to dismantle the entire wheel, that is, including the spokes. In any case, when you're dealing with the rear wheel, to be able to access the hub the freewheel has to be disassembled.

At this point, if the rims don't need to be replaced, it's time to check the tires. In conservative restoration, this step can be more complicated than you might imagine. Normally, the tires or tubulars need to be replaced not just for aesthetic reasons, but for functional reasons as well: the tread may be worn out or it may be deformed; sometimes the rubber has dried out. Unfortunately, for very old bicycles, let's say ones produced before the 1960s, it isn't easy to find the right tire on the market, not to mention that they're expensive. Keep in mind that today many companies produce models of tubulars and tires that look like the ones that were used in the past and, seeing the technological progress that has been made in recent years, they're an excellent alternative to the original ones, even though, generally speaking, they'll never have the same aesthetic impact. So if you're forced to make this choice, at least make sure they're the same type and color as the original ones so they'll go well with everything else. However, if the tires are even slightly acceptable, then the best thing to do is restore them. Both tires and tubulars can be cleaned with soap and a sponge, especially the canvas part.

On the other hand, you'll be forced to change the tire tubes, especially if you're replacing the tires. If you don't, you risk getting a flat.

As concerns tires and tubulars, a few words need to be said about measurements, which often create some confusion, especially for those of you who aren't experts, and for bikes other than road bikes, for example, women's, touring, and mountain bikes, as well as choppers. Usually all the information concerning size is embossed right on the tire, indicated in various ways. Three systems are used most often: the ETRTO (European Tire and Rim Technical Organization) system, the English system (in inches), and the French system (in millimeters). The first of these is perhaps the one used the most as well as being the clearest in terms of the information it provides—width size and the internal diameter—making it easier to correlate these measurements with the diameter of the rim.

Tubulars and clinchers for racing bicycles all have the same diameter: 28 inches. The width instead differs, and each width has its pros and cons. The range goes from a minimum of 19 to a maximum of 27 millimeters. The latter is the most popular width for "heroic" routes, with off-road tracks, where the strain is greater and the risk of getting a flat higher. Tubulars or tires measuring 19 or 20 millimeters, besides having less friction on the road, can also be inflated to a higher pressure, and they're obviously lighter. The measurements in the mid-range, from 22 to 25 millimeters, are the most common ones, and represent the right compromise between two extremes.

Lastly, I would like to stress that the wheels are a key component in creative restorations. This is especially true when it comes to fixed-gear bicycles, since the bicycle is practically stripped down. To improve the bike's appearance, besides the handlebar and saddle, the focus is on the wheels. There are all sorts of things to choose from in a project of this kind—rims for every taste, and a whole variety of hubs, spokes, and even nipples.

A 1950s Cilo. This is a great example of how wooden rims can have an impact on the appearance of the bike, giving it a retro look.

**The saddle** From a personal standpoint, the saddle is the part of the bicycle that intrigues me the most. Maybe it's the shape, or the materials it's made of, maybe it's that patina of wear that often distinguishes it, or its strong "artisanal" look. I think it partially also depends on the fact that leather saddles from the past had to be broken in, the owner had to make the saddle his or her own. By using it you made it fit your anatomy and this also meant going through a period of… aches. But besides this personal passion, it's a fact that when you restore a bike the saddle is one of the most important components.

In recent years, saddles, like other parts of the bicycle, have witnessed a technical evolution in materials and forms: shells and paddings have changed, as have the materials used for the cover. Saddles have also become increasingly lighter and more comfortable. But there is no comparison between a vintage saddle, with all its charm and beauty, and the ones manufactured today.

There are touring bike saddles, road bike saddles, track bike saddles, chopper saddles, saddles of all shapes and materials, cheap saddles and expensive saddles. Today, there are still companies that, having operated on the market for over a century, continue to produce very high-quality saddles with the same craftsmanship as in the past.

When restoring a saddle conservatively you need to check that it's still in good condition, especially that there aren't any tears in the shell. If the cover is made of leather, rubbing on a layer of cream or special grease will make it look brand new again. If, instead, the leather is misshapen, all you need to do is place the saddle in lukewarm water to soften it up and then put it back into shape with the help of a mold and a vise. If the shell is made of iron and has rusted, sand it the same way you sanded the iron crank arms in Chapter Four, and once you've eliminated the rust, brush some anti-corrosion oil over it for protection.

If instead the saddle has cuts or abrasions that are aesthetically unacceptable, then go ahead and replace it, making sure that the replacement saddle is from the same period the bike was made. In the past, bicycle catalogues included the brand and the model of the saddle assembled on the bike; however, if you don't have specific references you can replace it with something you like, as long as it's the same type as the original one and from the same period. It's easy to imagine that for very old bicycles, that is, ones produced before the 1960s, this becomes more complicated and the cost higher, but keep in mind that many companies still sell old models today: this is a good alternative to the original. For total restoration pay close attention to the condition of the saddle: if it's not close to perfect, then you'll want to replace it, because aesthetically it would make no sense to assemble a saddle that's not perfect on a frame that's been made to look brand new.

In creative restoration the saddle is an essential component for the overall success of the project, and usually this is why it's the part of the bike you invest the most money in, besides a new paint job for the frame. In the world of urban culture the bicycle has become a status symbol, an emblem of the right way to be and to live, and this is why fashion and cycling so often influence each other. There are lots of designers and artists who have created or collaborated on the production of special saddle models, the one bicycle component that best lends itself to this type of collaboration. Furthermore, touring bikes often come with tool bags, which can also be personalized.

A beautiful saddle always makes an impression and adds that special touch to the bike. And if you're careful about matching it with the handlebar cover, the overall results will be even more pleasing to the eye. The explosion of social media has brought to light many master artisans who know how to personalize both the handlebar and the saddle, so there are lots of solutions that can be adopted. All you need to do is research some of the social networks to find out just how many solutions are available. The more specific you get,

WHEELS, SADDLE, AND HANDLEBAR

the more you end up spending and the greater the personalization, especially when conservative restoration allows for that freedom of action.

An alternative for the person who can't spend much and maybe wants a particular cover is DIY. With a pinch of know-how you can repurpose a saddle simply by giving it a new cover. All you need is a pair of scissors, some fabric glue, and some clothespins to cover a saddle and get acceptable results. The freedom to choose a cover that's to your liking makes the project unique, not to mention the satisfaction you get from finishing

a job like this with your own two hands. In the end you'll have brought back to life an object that looked like it was ready to be thrown out. And if you're not sure you're capable of doing a good job you can always contact a saddlery or a professional upholsterer. (As always, make sure you get an estimate.)

In short, the saddle is perhaps the component that requires the greatest care as concerns choice, and that, along with the handlebar cover and the type of tires, contributes the most to the visual impact of a restored bike.

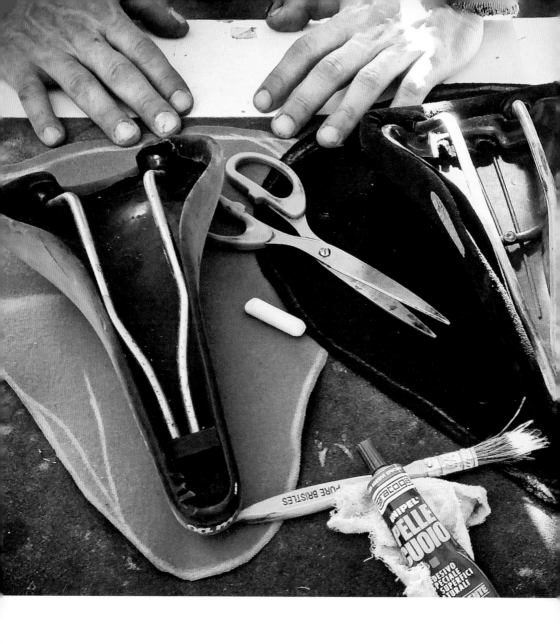

On pp. 196-99: This women's
bike clearly shows how the
wheels and the handlebar are
important from an aesthetic
standpoint.

# REGISTRO DELLE BICICLETTE EROICHE

## *L'Eroica* ®

N° PROGRESSIVO: *1315*

REGISTRAZIONE DEL    *4 Ottobre 2013*

| | | | |
|---|---|---|---|
| Marca | LEO | Modello | Corsa |
| Anno | 1957 | Matricola | |
| Telaio | Columbus | H telaio | |
| Colore | crema | Provenienza | Firenze |

Componenti   Manubrio, attacco Cinelli in acciaio cromato - serie di sterzo, cambio, deragliatore centrale, pedali, mozzi Campagnolo Gran Sport - freni Universal 51 - ingranaggio Simplex - pedivelle Magistroni - cerchi Nisi.

Note   Bicicletta usata da Gastone Nencini nel 1957.

Restaurata ☐   Conservata ☒   Stato   ☒ Ottimo   ☐ Buono   ☐ Sufficiente

# THE REGISTRY OF HISTORICAL BICYCLES OF THE EROICA

*Aldo Pacini*

—

One of the organizers of the Eroica and a member of the Commission that evaluates bicycles for the Registry of Historical Bicycles

I approached the Eroica for the first time in 2000, when I was asked to chair it, as vice-president of the UISP National Cycling League, and I fell in love with it immediately.

My total involvement in the event only came about starting from 2007, when Furio Giannini, a close collaborator of Giancarlo Brocci, the organizer from the time of its first edition in 1997, asked me and my friend and master bicycle restorer Medardo Fioresi if we wanted to deal with the Registry of Heroic Bicycles he intended to set up. He spoke to us in general terms and gave us broad freedom of choice in terms of organization.

We got straight down to work, and the first thing we did was look for anyone who might have the necessary skills and passion to be a member of the group. I'd been spending time in that world for several years, so it wasn't too hard to get the collaboration of the "right" people: Irio Tommasini, a well-known frame builder as well as a collector of vintage bicycles was the first to be contacted, and he accepted enthusiastically, just as Paolo Cavazzuti, a restorer and collector, was also glad to join the company. The following October our adventure could finally get off the ground.

The aim was a simple one: to collect images, news, and data relating to "road and non-road" bikes built before 1987 and still in working order, for the purpose of making their uniqueness, their history, and above all their unique beauty both known and appreciated. We chose 1987 because it was the year when pedals with the new Look-type fittings ultimately took over from the traditional "toe-clips," an emblematic sign—along with brake cables running along the inside of the frame, and gear levers on the handlebar next to the ones for the brakes instead of on the frame—of the transition from the "heroic" cycling of

olden times to the modern, hyper-technological kind.

Anyone can ask for his or her bike to be added to the Registry, submitting it to an evaluation by a board of experts whose job is to judge the legitimacy of the application. For each bicycle, a form has to be filled out specifying the brand, model, year of construction, color, size, and serial number of the frame, and, if known, the provenance. Also indicated are any details concerning the components (group, brakes, handlebars, saddle, etc.), besides other remarks deemed to be of interest for classification purposes. The form is completed with a photograph and the words "Restored Bicycle" or "Conserved Bicycle," accompanied, in the latter case, by an evaluation of its state of conservation (excellent, good, satisfactory).

Today, the Registry numbers a few thousand bicycles, including some absolute heirlooms, like the Leo with which Gastone Nencini won the Giro d'Italia in 1957.

Joining this project was a veritable journey into a new world, which has given me the chance to measure up to cyclists and champions past and present, both as concerns the mechanical details and the riding techniques on dirt roads. I have also been able to evaluate bicycles dating from the late nineteenth century to the 1980s, appreciating the craftsmanship and ingeniousness that was required of past manufacturers in order to make up for the lack of technology.

New challenges and new adventures await us… For example, there is talk of extending the Registry to the various "Eroiche" that are now taking place all around the world. And when I look at the many imitations that have surfaced in the past few years, all I can say is, to borrow Brocci's words, "every copy adds value to the original."

**The handlebar**  I've always thought there's something erotic about a bicycle handlebar. The various shapes it's been given over the past century have always had a special design and profile, which to my mind accentuates the bike's sensuality. If Picasso had painted a bicycle, I'm sure he would have left his mark on the handlebar. If we look at the angles and the widths of certain shapes used in the past, especially before the 1940s, we can see there's a predominant trait, something sexy... Curves just hinted at or extreme bends have a strong visual impact and transmit to the metal those elegant and sinuous shapes that you want to grip vigorously. If you look at the naked elegance of a track bicycle, especially a vintage one, you'll see that the beauty of its appearance depends on the shape of the handlebar. In the past, especially in the 1980s, futuristic solutions were adopted with handlebar clamps very close to the front wheel. All these experiments were linked to the first aerodynamic studies, sometimes with questionable results, other times with "outrageous" ones.

Materials, bends, handlebar stems have changed and improved a lot over the years. Every type of bicycle has its "own" handlebar. There are specific bends for touring bikes, mountain bikes, racing bikes... When you restore a bike conservatively sometimes it's hard to maintain the handlebar model of the original bike, also because the differences aren't always that obvious. For very old bicycles, the ones from the 1920s and '30s, identifying them can be a real challenge. The most extreme bends have become a much sought after object by collectors.

The first thing you need to consider is that until the 1930s handlebar were mostly made of iron. Aluminum made its appearance in France toward the end of the 1930s, with the introduction of duraluminum in aeronautic factories. Moreover, at the start of the century, the stem and the handlebar were forged in a single piece and it was only from the 1930s that the two pieces started being produced separately, giving cyclists the chance to adjust the stem depending on their sizes. In the 1940s the handlebar stem underwent some interesting developments in terms of both the material used, such as aluminum, and the shape, but it was in the 1950s that there was a sweeping change, especially as concerned design. A higher-up posture called for a change in the position of the clamp on the upper part of the handlebar. Gentle,

downward-tending curves were thus replaced by straighter lines that allowed the cyclist to place his or her hands on the top of the handlebar, guaranteeing a more comfortable "drive." The width also changed, and the handlebar became shorter and more compact, to the great advantage of the maneuverability of the bike itself. A new series of innovations, which would radically change the look of the handlebar, came about in the late 1980s. Among the most conspicuous, at least in racing bikes, were the external housings which were now being bundled together along the inside of the handlebar.

In parallel with the shape of the handlebar, there was also a change in tapes and covers. From the start of the century to the 1920s, the handlebar was substantially unfinished, but it did have grips. Later, the first cotton fabric tape appeared on the market, which remained the most common cover until the 1960s. Not until the 1970s did the choice expand, with the introduction of shiny nylon tapes or more padded plastic ones, whose material was known as "pelten." In those same years, an elegant and refined leather cover was patented as well. This involved sewing the leather directly onto the handlebar, giving it a unique, luxury look.

Choosing the right tape, like the right handlebar, is very important when you're restoring a bike conservatively. One of the most common errors is that of allowing yourself to use whatever tape you want. Every period in history has its own tape, and this has to be taken into account. Although it might seem to be an irrelevant detail, in the end it's more important than many others.

An interesting way of protecting the handlebar, especially employed by the French since the 1930s, is the use of shellac to fix and waterproof the fabric tape. In addition to preserving the tape for a long time, shellac brings out the beauty of the fabric and accentuates the colors, modifying them depending on the initial color of the tape. If you start from a yellow tape, for example, you'll get a light brown one. Orange turns to dark brown, and red to deep burgundy.

The effect is beautiful, but don't use this technique just because you feel like it. It's especially suitable if you're restoring a certain type of French bicycle, normally used in *randonneuses*. In Japan, where this type of cycling is still widespread today, using shellac is very popular and greatly appreciated because of its excellent fixative property, and

A procedure for the protection of the handlebar, especially used by the French from the late 1930s, was that of covering it with shellac. You'll need to buy shellac in thin pieces or already dissolved in alcohol, protective goggles, gloves, a brush, a bowl, and some masking tape. After applying the tape to the handlebar, attach it and mask the parts that are exposed (photo 1). Now use a brush to apply the first layer of shellac, letting the fabric absorb it thoroughly (photo 2). After the first coat, let it rest for at least eight hours (photo 3), then repeat six/eight more times at one-hour intervals. When you've finished, let the handlebar rest for two whole days (photo 4).

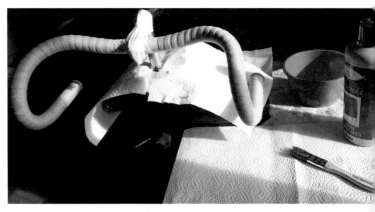

because of the way it beautifies the tape, making it as elegant as skin.

Wheels, saddle, and handlebar: three key elements in every bicycle, to be evaluated carefully when you're restoring an old bike, but above all to be considered as they relate to each other, creating the right combinations from a historic standpoint, and appealing ones from an aesthetic one. Despite the fact that the variants in the original colors of the tires, tapes, and saddles were at one time limited, even with conservative restoration you have a certain freedom to choose and consequently a fair number of color combinations.

If you're restoring your bike creatively, instead, the choice of colors today is endless.

We have come to the end of our wonderful journey, and every stop we made along the way helped us to discover an exciting "place": bicycle restoration. Now it's up to you to get some practice. When you've finally finished the job, whatever the results, you should feel satisfied that you may have gotten your hands dirty, but you've also cleansed your soul.

The effect of the application of shellac on tapes of different colors. This gives the tape a luxury, refined, and, at the same time, vintage look. Note how the wheels, handlebar, and saddle, the three components discussed in this chapter, manage to "dress" the whole bicycle and draw all the attention.

Texts by Gianluca Zaghi
Book design and layout by Heartfelt.it
English translation by Sylvia Adrian Notini

Contributions by
Helio Ascari, Luciano Berruti, Giancarlo Brocci, Wesley Hatakeyama,
Aldo Pacini, Stelio Rossi, Greg Softley, Mike Wolfe.

Gianluca Zaghi may be contacted at:
Istagram: vintagespeedbicycles
Flickr.com: VSB Vintage Speed Bicycles
Ebay: vintagespeedbicycles and for parts campyhunter11
Email: gianlucazaghi@sunrise.ch

Photo credits
All of the photographs are by © Gianluca Zaghi, except for:
p. 8: Dario Garofalo (© Consorzio Chianti Classico)
p. 17: Claudio Bertarelli
pp. 24, 25: Heritage Cappelletti Family
p. 40: Jacques Dequeker
pp. 41, 42: Patrick Farrell
p. 43: Patrick Farrell (the bike); Jacques Dequeker (Helio Ascari)
pp. 58, 59: Ferdinando Capecchi
p. 69: Paolo Martelli
p. 107: Tracey Hatakeyama
p. 152: Greg Softley
p. 206: Lisa Martini

The Publisher remains at the disposal of claimants
for any sources not identified.

www.electa.it

Distributed in English throughout the World
by Rizzoli international Publications Inc.
300 Park Avenue South
New York, NY 10010, USA

**ISO 9001**
Mondadori Electa S.p.A. is certified for the Quality
Management System by Bureau Veritas Italia S.p.A.,
in compliance with UNI EN ASO 9001: 2008.

**This book respects the environment**
The paper used was produced using wood from forests managed
to strict environmental standards; the companies involved
guarantee sustainable production certified environmentally.

This volume was printed in August 2017 at Elcograf S.p.A.,
Via Mondadori 15, Verona
Printed in Italy